RELATIONSHIP PROCESSES AND RESILIENCE IN CHILDREN WITH INCARCERATED PARENTS

EDITED BY

Julie Poehlmann

J. Mark Eddy

Patricia J. Bauer
Series Editor*

MONOGRAPHS OF THE SOCIETY FOR RESEARCH IN CHILD DEVELOPMENT

Serial No. 308, Vol. 78, No. 3, 2013

*This monograph was accepted under the editorship of W. Andrew Collins.

WILEY   *Boston, Massachusetts*   *Oxford, United Kingdom*

RELATIONSHIP PROCESSES AND RESILIENCE IN CHILDREN WITH INCARCERATED PARENTS

CONTENTS

ABSTRACT*

Children with incarcerated parents are at risk for a variety of problematic outcomes, yet research has rarely examined protective factors or resilience processes that might mitigate such risk in this population. In this volume, we present findings from five new studies that focus on child- or family-level resilience processes in children with parents currently or recently incarcerated in jail or prison. In the first study, empathic responding is examined as a protective factor against aggressive peer relations for 210 elementary school age children of incarcerated parents. The second study further examines socially aggressive behaviors with peers, with a focus on teasing and bullying, in a sample of 61 children of incarcerated mothers. Emotion regulation is examined as a possible protective factor. The third study contrasts children's placement with maternal grandmothers versus other caregivers in a sample of 138 mothers incarcerated in a medium security state prison. The relation between a history of positive attachments between mothers and grandmothers and the current cocaregiving alliance are of particular interest. The fourth study examines coparenting communication in depth on the basis of observations of 13 families with young children whose mothers were recently released from jail. Finally, in the fifth study, the proximal impacts of a parent management training intervention on individual functioning and family relationships are investigated in a diverse sample of 359 imprisoned mothers and fathers. Taken together, these studies further our understanding of resilience processes in children of incarcerated parents and their families and set the groundwork for further research on child development and family resilience within the context of parental involvement in the criminal justice system.

---

*This monograph was accepted under the editorship of W. Andrew Collins.

I. INTRODUCTION AND CONCEPTUAL FRAMEWORK

Julie Poehlmann and J. Mark Eddy

Since 1991, the number of U.S. children with an imprisoned parent has increased by 80%, affecting more than 1.7 million children in 2007 (Glaze & Maruschak, 2008). Estimates also suggest that millions of additional children have a parent in jail (Kemper & Rivara, 1993; Western & Wildeman, 2009), although the actual number of affected children is unknown because this information is not systematically collected by correctional, school, or other service systems. Although these numbers are staggering, they are hardly unexpected, given that the U.S. incarcerates more people than any country in the world (Pew Charitable Trusts, 2008). Incarceration rates rose dramatically during the 1980s and 1990s, related to changes in policies that not only decreased judicial discretion regarding incarceration and sentence length but also heightened the focus on the punishment, rather than the reform, of drug offenders (Austin & Irwin, 2001; The Sentencing Project, 2009). The result is an unprecedented reliance on incarceration. Today, more than 1 in 100 adults in the United States are in jail or prison, including 1 in 30 men between the ages of 20 and 34 years (Pew Charitable Trusts, 2008), and most prisoners have at least one minor child (Glaze & Maruschak, 2008).

Incarceration is not equally distributed across the population. Disparities in incarceration rates based on race and educational attainment have resulted in a concentration of incarceration among disadvantaged individuals, families, and communities (Western & Wildeman, 2009). Sadly, these disparities have resulted in large numbers of African American children having a parent in prison or jail. Indeed, African American children were 7.5 times more likely to experience the imprisonment of a parent than white children in 2007 (Glaze & Maruschak, 2008). The disparity is even greater when examining the experience of parental incarceration throughout

*Corresponding author: Julie Poehlmann, School of Human Ecology and Waisman Center, 1500 Highland Ave., University of Wisconsin, Madison, WI 53705, email: poehlmann@waisman.wisc.edu

1

childhood, rather than at one point in time. For example, by age 14, 50.5% of African American children born to a father who dropped out of high school will experience his imprisonment, whereas this is true for only 7.2% of white children (Wildeman, 2009).

Risk, Resilience, and Relationships

Children of incarcerated parents are about twice as likely as their peers to exhibit antisocial behavior and other mental health problems (Murray, Farrington, Sekol, & Olsen, 2009). A wide range of risk factors related to these childhood problems is present in the lives of many children of incarcerated parents, including poverty, parental substance abuse, and repeated changes in caregivers and schools. Disrupted family relationships are common, especially for children whose incarcerated mothers cared for children on a daily basis prior to imprisonment (Poehlmann, 2005a). Historically, keen awareness of the potentially serious impacts of parental separation on child adjustment has led to the application of an attachment perspective to studies of this population (e.g., Makariev & Shaver, 2010; Murray & Murray, 2010; Poehlmann, 2010). However, numerous other perspectives have been considered in recent years, including family systems theory, social learning theory, ecological theory, and lifespan development theory, as evidenced by the various papers in this volume and in other recently published collections (e.g., Eddy & Poehlmann, 2010). Central to each of these perspectives is the importance of parent–child and family relationships and their correlates in delineating possible pathways toward competence or pathology.

Although theories focusing on parent–child and family relationships clearly point to certain resilience processes that could be examined for children with incarcerated parents (e.g., relationships with alternate caregivers, development of empathy, family-level security), much of the literature focusing on this population has documented risks and emphasized negative developmental outcomes in children (e.g., Murray et al., 2009). However, children do not exhibit uniform reactions to significant risk or adversity, and some children function well despite their experience of parental incarceration. Indeed, many children of incarcerated parents show resilience, or the process of successful adaptation in the face of significant adversity (Luthar, Cicchetti, & Becker, 2000). It is crucial that the emphasis on disrupted family relationships and multiple risks in children with incarcerated parents does not overshadow our examination of possible resilience processes in these children.

Masten (2001) has argued that resilience in the presence of adversity is a relatively ordinary or even expected process for children when normative human adaptational systems remain intact and protective, such as positive

2

family relationships, effective parenting, and normative cognitive development. Although maintenance of normative systems, especially related to parenting and family relationships, is extremely challenging for many children and families impacted by parental incarceration, understanding resilience processes in children with incarcerated parents is critical for the design of prevention and intervention programs. Few studies have examined resilience processes in children of jailed or imprisoned parents, and even fewer have examined interpersonal relationships in relation to resilience in this population. Most longitudinal studies examining children's development or behaviors in the context of parental incarceration have relied on secondary analysis of data collected for other purposes, and thus do not provide information that is specific to the experience of parental incarceration (e.g., separation from parents or other caregivers, relationships with alternative caregivers, social stigma or peer teasing related to parental incarceration, contact between children and their incarcerated parents). New data are needed to examine protective factors and resilience processes in children with incarcerated parents, especially in the areas of interpersonal relationships.

In the present volume, the authors apply a resilience framework to examine processes associated with parent–child, intergenerational family, and peer relationships, including the development of empathy, emotion regulation, maternal attachments to their own mothers, and positive communication processes during coparenting interactions. Although much research links these relationship processes to the well-being of children in low- and high-risk groups, including children who have experienced maltreatment or those who are in foster care, few studies have examined such processes in children with incarcerated parents (see Poehlmann & Eddy, 2010). Each study in the present volume applies interpersonal relationship constructs and theories to the research at hand in order to understand emerging resilience in children of incarcerated parents.

Specificity of Terminology

When we refer to children with incarcerated parents, who do we mean? In this volume and in our previous writing (e.g., Eddy & Poehlmann, 2010; Poehlmann et al., 2010), we have used the term "parental incarceration" to refer to parents who are in prison or jail. This includes current incarceration in jail or prison, or incarceration that occurs during one's childhood. Similarly, Murray and Farrington (2005) used the term to refer to fathers who were incarcerated in local or federal institutions at some point during their child's first 10 years of life, and Dallaire and Wilson (2010) used the term to refer to parents currently in a community jail. Some scholars

3

have combined children of jailed and imprisoned parents in their analyses (Murray et al., 2009). But how do prisons and jails differ? Jails are locally operated correctional facilities that confine persons before or after adjudication (BJS, 2010). Jail sentences are usually 1 year or less, usually result from misdemeanor convictions. Sentences to state prison are generally more than 1 year and typically the result of felony convictions, although this varies by state. Six states currently have integrated correctional systems that combine jails and prisons (BJS, 2010). Compared to prisons, jails are often located closer to the incarcerated individual's family members, possibly affecting visitation frequency and family processes. Compared to state prisons, there are fewer federal prisons; federal prisoners are under the legal authority of the U.S. federal government (BJS, 2010) and they are often located far from the incarcerated individual's family. Because of myriad differences between jail and prison settings and populations, and their potentially different effects on children, precision is important in defining samples of incarcerated parents.

Some scholars have conceptualized "parental incarceration" more broadly than the definition presented above, emphasizing the importance of other forms of current or past parental contact with the criminal justice system (e.g., arrest, probation, parole) for children's well-being. For example, Phillips, Erkanli, Costello, and Angold (2006) used the term to refer to past maternal contact with the criminal justice system, whereas other scholars have emphasized the possible negative effects of maternal arrest on children (Phillips & Erkanli, 2008; Shlafer, Poehlmann, & Donelan-McCall, 2012). As more is learned about the effects of current or past parental incarceration on children or specific effects of parental arrest, conviction, or parole, specificity is needed in defining the samples under study. Without this specificity, it will be difficult to discern whether there are certain risks associated with parental incarceration in prison or jail, or whether having a parent incarcerated is simply a general risk marker for children and families. Given this concern, each chapter in the present volume includes definitions of the samples under study, including whether mothers or fathers are currently incarcerated or recently released from jail or from prison.

This Volume

New data are of critical importance to answer basic questions regarding interpersonal relationship processes that may serve risk or protective functions for children of incarcerated parents. This monograph brings together five new studies examining family and peer relationship processes in relation to resilience in children with incarcerated parents. Although each study has unique strengths, they share several common themes, including

4

examination of resilience processes in the context of relationships as well as the importance of processes such as emotional regulation, individual and family-level communication, and empathy in family and peer contexts.

The first study, by Dallaire and Zeman, examines children's peer relations and behavior problems in several groups, including children with incarcerated parents and children separated from their parents for other reasons. Findings indicate that children who experience current or past parental incarceration engage in more aggressive behaviors compared to children who experience other forms of parental separation. However, data show that children's empathic responding to peers functions as a protective factor regarding the experience of negative peer relations in elementary school children with incarcerated parents.

The second study, by Myers et al., further examines socially aggressive behaviors with peers, especially bullying, in children of incarcerated mothers attending a summer camp. Mentor-reported data indicate that better emotion regulation predicts less bullying in children of incarcerated mothers. Thus, emotion regulation can be viewed as a factor that may contribute to resilience in this high risk group.

The third study, by Loper and Novero Clarke, examines coparenting alliances and mother–child contact in a relatively large sample of families with imprisoned mothers, contrasting intergenerational relationships when children are cared for by their maternal grandmothers with families of children who are cared for by other caregivers. The study documents a significant association between incarcerated mothers' positive attachments to their own mothers, adaptive coparenting alliances with caregivers, and higher levels of mother–child contact during maternal incarceration for grandmother-headed families. These findings suggest that a positive mother–grandmother relationship is a potential protective factor for children of incarcerated mothers who are placed with their maternal grandmothers.

The fourth study, by McHale et al., provides a detailed description of the dynamics of mother–grandmother coparenting alliances in families following a mother's jail stay. The study provides data from observations of coparenting behaviors between formerly incarcerated mothers and the grandmothers who cared for children while mothers were away. Observations occurred during home visits during the early weeks after the mother's release, revealing a wide range of triangular dynamics between mother, grandmother, and child. Although a subset of families exhibited clinical levels of disconnection or conflict, more common was cooperative coparenting, sometimes led by the grandmother and sometimes led by the mother. The women's capacity to mutually support one another's efforts and provide needed scaffolding for the young children following the mother's community reentry may be a critical resource, particularly for families in which children exhibit internalizing or externalizing behavior problems.

5

The final study, by J. M. Eddy et al., examines outcomes from the first large-scale randomized controlled trial of a parent management training intervention for mothers and fathers incarcerated in state prisons. The theory-based, strengths-focused intervention was designed to improve the adjustment of incarcerated parents and the quality of their relationships with children and children's caregivers. Relative to controls, intervention participants reported positive outcomes in numerous areas of parental functioning immediately following the intervention, including less depression and parenting stress, more positive parent–child contact, and better relationships with the child's caregiver.

Additional studies with characteristics such as those in this volume are vitally needed to inform practices and policies relevant to children of incarcerated parents. Each study examines issues related to the importance of interpersonal relationship processes in different contexts for children of incarcerated parents and their families. Each study highlights issues related to child and family resilience. Families in which mothers and fathers are incarcerated are included; participants come from a variety of racial/ethnic and economic backgrounds; and potential resilience processes in children of different ages are considered. Taken together, the findings from these studies lead to a deeper understanding of, and a greater respect for, family and peer relationships and the well-being of children within the challenging context of parental incarceration. We hope that the information in this volume not only assists lay people and professionals as they work with and make decisions about children affected by parental incarceration, but also stimulates further high-quality research on resilience within this high-risk population of children.

II. EMPATHY AS A PROTECTIVE FACTOR FOR CHILDREN WITH INCARCERATED PARENTS

Danielle H. Dallaire and Janice L. Zeman

A growing body of research has demonstrated that children with an incarcerated parent are at risk for a myriad of problematic behaviors, including internalizing and externalizing behavior problems (Wilbur et al., 2007) and academic difficulties (Trice & Brewster, 2004). Furthermore, they may also be at increased risk for continuing an intergeneration cycle of crime and incarceration (Dallaire, 2007). A recent meta-analysis found that children who experienced parental incarceration were twice as likely as peers to exhibit antisocial behavior problems and mental health problems (Murray et al., 2009). Despite increased empirical attention devoted to studying the effects of parental incarceration on children's development, few studies have examined protective factors that may buffer children from stress associated with parental incarceration. Much of what is known about how parental incarceration impacts children and families originates from secondary analysis of data sets not intended to test questions related to how children and families cope with a current parental incarceration (e.g., Aaron & Dallaire, 2010; Cho, 2009; Dallaire, 2007; Phillips & Erkanli, 2008). In contrast, the current study was designed to examine children's prosocial empathic behavior as a factor that may protect children from engaging in aggressive peer relations in a sample of children who have a parent currently incarcerated.

Research has demonstrated that children with incarcerated parents face numerous challenges in their caregiving environments, including poverty (Western & Wildeman, 2009), harsh and potentially abusive parenting behavior (Phillips, Burns, Wagner, & Barth, 2004), and highly stressed caregivers (Mackintosh, Myers, & Kennon, 2006). A significant issue in the literature concerns the operationalization of parental incarceration. As discussed in the Introduction to this volume, "parental incarceration" is an umbrella term typically used to refer to parents who are imprisoned or jailed,

*Corresponding author: Danielle Dallaire, Department of Psychology, College of William and Mary, P.O. Box 8795, Williamsburg, VA 23187, email: dhdall@wm.edu

although some scholars use the term more broadly, indicating other forms of contact with the criminal justice system (e.g., arrest, parole). It is unclear whether these different definitions reflect unique or similar experiences for affected children. As such, greater specificity should be employed when referencing children with incarcerated parents. In the present study, we differentiate between children who are experiencing a current parental incarceration in jail or prison from those who have experienced a past parental incarceration and those who have experienced past or current separation from parents for reasons other than incarceration.

Attachment theory offers one of several possible frameworks (e.g., temperament, behavioral) for explaining why children with incarcerated parents may be an at-risk population and it can delineate the processes through which pathways to resilience may be fostered (Poehlmann, 2010). Poehlmann (2005a) found that most children separated from their imprisoned mothers maintained representations of insecure relationships with the incarcerated mother and current caregiver, although a stable caregiving situation was found to be a protective factor. Clearly, parental incarceration may negatively impact children's ability to form and maintain stable, secure attachment relationships with the incarcerated parent. Attachment theory suggests that, to the extent that children with incarcerated parents can form or maintain a secure, organized attachment relationship with the incarcerated parent or another caregiver, they may be protected from some of the other risks associated with the experience of parental incarceration. In the low-risk sample of families who participated in the National Institute of Child Health and Human Development (NICHD) Study of Early Childcare, attachment security has been found to protect children against the experience of contextual risk (e.g., low marital support, Belsky & Fearon, 2002) and mother's experience of various life stressors (e.g., job loss, moving, birth of a new child, Dallaire & Weinraub, 2007). However, similar work has not been conducted with children of incarcerated parents.

Attachment security has been thought to promote the development of empathy in children through engendering emotional awareness and empathic responding (Kerns, 2008; Thompson, 2008). Sensitive and responsive maternal behaviors promote both attachment security (see de Wolff & van IJzendoorn, 1997) and empathy in children (Robinson & Little, 1994). Insecurely attached children have shown less empathy than their securely attached counterparts (Kestenbaum, Farber, & Sroufe, 1989). Grusec and Davido (2010) speculate that the caregiving behaviors that promote attachment security (e.g., sensitive responsiveness) are the specific types of parenting behaviors and socialization strategies that promote empathic prosocial responding in children. A potential mechanism whereby maternal sensitivity predicts to empathy is modeling and social learning (Kiang, Moreno, & Robinson, 2004).

Empathy, as defined by Cohen and Strayer (1996) is "the ability to understand and share in another's emotional state or context" (p. 988), and it is considered critical for adaptive socio-emotional development (Bornstein, 2005). Previous research has demonstrated that empathy is an important component of children's prosocial behaviors and peer relations. For example, in a study of elementary school age children, prosocial children displayed greater empathic awareness than both bullies and victims of relational or physical aggression (Warden & Mackinnon, 2003), illustrating the strong connection between empathy and prosocial behavior. Empathy is also related to antisocial behavior. Specifically, in a sample of adolescent male criminal offenders, low empathy scores were related to psychopathy, one of the most stable predictors of persistent and serious criminal behavior (Holmqvist, 2008), and in adulthood, low levels of empathy have been linked to criminality (Jolliffe & Farrington, 2004). In contrast, self-reported empathy was negatively associated with self-reports of both aggressive and delinquent behaviors in adolescents (de Kemp, Overbeek, de Wied, Engels, & Scholte, 2007). Given that children with incarcerated parents are at increased risk for continuing an intergenerational cycle of crime, and empathy is associated with criminal behavior, empathy may be an important moderator of the relation between parental incarceration and behavioral problems that affected children display. Further, children who have a parent currently incarcerated likely experience considerable stress that places a burden on their coping skills, including their ability to respond to others in an empathic prosocial way. That is, under conditions of stress children may have few emotional reserves to use and cannot afford to expend any of them to meet the needs of others in prosocial ways, as their energy must be spent toward meeting their own socioemotional regulatory needs and goals (Compas, 1987). It is possible that when the parent is no longer incarcerated, these children may have more emotional resources in combination with parental modeling and socialization of empathy to then display more prosocial behaviors to their peers (Vinik, Almas, & Grusec, 2011).

Previous research has demonstrated that children with incarcerated parents or parents otherwise involved in the criminal justice system are likely to be cared for by caregivers who are stressed (Arditti, Lambert-Shute, & Joest, 2003; Mackintosh et al., 2006), and who may be more likely to use harsh and punitive parenting behaviors (Phillips, et al., 2004; Phillips, Erkanli, Costello, et al., 2006) than other families. Stressed caregivers who engage in harsh parenting behaviors may be less likely to model prosocial empathic responses to others' distress and in fact may model more aggressive behaviors that may negatively impact children's peer relations. Furthermore, a current, as opposed to past parental incarceration, may acutely stress the caregiver resulting in more quick-tempered parenting behaviors. Although less than half of parents incarcerated in state prisons report living with a child before their incarceration (Glaze & Marushak, 2008), a current incarceration can still produce detrimental effects on a child and the family system. Prior to incarceration, that parent and the family may have provided social and financial support to the child's primary caregiver. The absence of such support when the parent is incarcerated can contribute to the level of stress a caregiver experiences which then affects his or her parenting skills.

One of the outcomes associated with parental incarceration that has received limited empirical attention, yet represents a key developmental milestone, concerns children's peer relations. Many children and youth who experience parental incarceration report feeling isolated from peers because of their unique parental situation (Nesmith & Ruhland, 2008). Other research has found children with incarcerated parents to be at risk for associating with deviant and delinquent peers (e.g., Hanlon, Blatchley, Bennett-Sears, O'Grady, & Callaman, 2005; Huebner & Gustafson, 2007). Delinquent peer group affiliation is a serious risk factor for this population of children because aggressive behavior and substance use often take place within the adolescent peer group context (e.g., Brendgen, Vitaro, & Bukowski, 2000). In contrast, positive peer relations may be an important protective factor for children impacted by parental incarceration because high-quality and supportive friendships buffer children from stressful experiences at school (e.g., Ladd, Kochenderfer, & Coleman, 1996) and provide additional support during stressful life events (e.g., Windle, 1992).

In comparison to the number of studies that have examined risks in the lives of children with incarcerated parents, few have examined protective factors. Myers and colleagues have championed this approach in a series of studies conducted at a summer camp for children with incarcerated mothers. They found that hope (Hagen, Myers, & Mackintosh, 2005), social support (Hagen & Myers, 2003), and emotion regulation skills (Lotze, Ravindran, & Myers, 2010) may protect against the development of internalizing and externalizing behaviors. Unfortunately, these studies did not have comparison groups of children who did not experience parental incarceration or other forms of parental separation or adversity, making it difficult to determine whether the findings result from parental incarceration status or some other variable. Further, it is unclear whether certain factors such as positive peer relations and empathic responding may operate to protect against the development of these types of problematic outcomes.

Present Study

Using an ethnically diverse, public school–based sample of elementary-school-age children, we placed children into six groups based on their guardian-reported history of separation from their parents, including those with no history of parental separation, those with varying experiences with current and past parental incarceration, and those separated from parents for reasons other than incarceration (i.e., military deployment). We compared these groups on their empathic behavior and in relation to peer reports of aggressive behaviors. Whereas prior research focusing on the effects of incarceration on children has tended to rely solely on mother- or child-report of functioning using paper-and-pencil assessment tools, we utilized multiple reporters, including parent- and child-reports of empathy, plus peer ratings of aggressive peer relations. We also created a behavioral task designed to elicit comforting behavior from the child to a stranger (i.e., research assistant) as a measure of empathy.

Using previous research as a guide, we tested three hypotheses. First, we hypothesized that children with a parent currently incarcerated would be rated as less empathic, display less comforting behavior, and obtain higher ratings of peer-reported aggression than children who did not experience current or prior parental incarceration or separation for other reasons. Second, we hypothesized that the effect of a current parental incarceration would contribute uniquely to the prediction of children's empathy and peer-rated aggression over and above the influence of demographic factors (child age, gender, parental education, and income), and the effect of separation (past and current) for nonincarceration reasons, as well as past incarceration. Third, we hypothesized that children's empathy would moderate the relation between a current parental incarceration and aggressive peer relations, thus functioning as a protective factor.

METHOD

Participants

Participants with complete data included 210 elementary school children (44% male) in grades 2–5 ($M_{age} = 9.08$, $SD = 1.10$, 91.6–141.6 months) and their parents/guardians. Children were predominately African American (77%), 13% were Caucasian, and 10% reported multiple ethnicities. Participating parent/guardians were children's mothers (87%), grand-mothers (5.5%), and fathers (4.5%). Family incomes ranged from less than $10,000 (17.5%) to over $100,000 (2.0%) with the modal response being between $30,000 and $40,000 (13.0%). Education levels ranged from 8th grade or less (1%) to some education after a master's degree (2%), with the modal response being completion of high school (56.4%).

Procedure

After obtaining institutional review board approval from the authors' university and the participating school district, children and their parent/

guardian were recruited to participate by sending letters to all 2nd–5th grade children at two elementary schools in a mid-Atlantic city with high levels of crime and poverty. In total, 750 children were eligible to participate with a 68% return rate; of those returning consents, 88% of parents/guardians ($N = 450$) consented to allow their child to participate and 66% agreed to participate themselves by completing a questionnaire packet in the mail. For various reasons, including time constraints, child lack of interest, or children moving, complete data were obtained for 435 children (97%) of the initial 450 children with signed parental/guardian consents. Of the 297 parents/guardians who agreed to participate, 210 (71%) returned a completed questionnaire packet, and thus, the final sample size was 210 parent–child dyads. Parental participation rates did not differ by grade or child gender.

Children with parental permission were individually interviewed at school in a private location during nonacademic times (e.g., gym class, homeroom). After giving verbal assent, children were assigned at random to a male ($n = 3$) or female ($n = 10$) Caucasian research assistant to complete a 30-min interview that included Bryant's Index of Empathy for Children and Adolescents (BIECA) as well as the observational assessment of empathy. Interviewers were trained in study procedures by the authors to assure standardization of study protocols. During a second session that occurred approximately 1-month later, the peer aggression sociometric was administered (along with other measures) in groups of five classmates, with appropriate privacy precautions. Children received small toys for participating, whereas parents/guardians received a $20 gift card for returning their completed packet.

Measures

Parental Incarceration and Separation From Parents

Parents answered questions about parental separation and incarceration in prison or jail through a questionnaire designed for this study. Based on their responses to these questions, children were classified as belonging to one of the following six groups: (a) No Separation (NoS): According to parents/guardians, 54 children (27%) never experienced a separation from a parent; (b) Current Incarceration (CI): 24 (12%) were experiencing a current parental incarceration in prison or jail; (c) Past Incarceration (PI): 22 children (11%) experienced a past parental incarceration in prison or jail; (d) Current Separation but No Incarceration (CS-NoI): 51 children (25%) were currently separated from at least one parent for nonincarceration reasons; (e) Past Separation but No Incarceration (PS-NoI): 18 children (9%) had experienced a past separation for nonincarceration reasons; and (f) Past Incarceration and Current Separation not due to parental incarceration (PICS-NoI): 34 children (17%) experienced a past parental incarceration and were currently separated from a parent for reasons other than incarceration. Besides parental incarceration, common reasons for separation from parents included marital separation or divorce (30%), parental work commitments (including military deployment, 23%) and other family commitments (e.g., taking care of a sick relative, 16%).

Empathy

Child report. Empathic behavior was assessed using the 22-item BIECA (Bryant, 1982). Children respond to each item on a dichotomous scale. Reliability (Bryant, 1982) and validity have been established with total BIECA scores inversely related to antisocial behaviors (e.g., de Kemp et al., 2007; Holmqvist, 2008). Other research (de Weid et al., 2007), however, has indicated that a 2-factor solution is a better fit to the data. We conducted principal components analyses with varimax rotation that extracted two components and accounted for 22.33% of the variance (see Table 1 for item loadings, eigenvalues, and internal consistency). The first scale reflected children's empathic sadness in response to others' distress, whereas the second scale represents children's attitudes toward children who display emotion. Given our study's goals, only the first component was retained for use, and a summed score was created, with girls scoring higher than boys, $t(200) = 3.86$, $p < .001$.

Parent report. Parents/guardians reported on children's empathic behaviors with peers using the Prosocial with Peers subscale of the revised Child Behavior Scale (Ladd & Proffitt, 1996). Using a 3-point scale (0 = not true, 1 = sometimes true, 2 = often true), parents rated nine items (i.e., "this child seems concerned when other children are distressed"). Validity has been demonstrated through its associations with observations of children's classroom prosocial behavior, fewer observations of aggressive interactions in the classroom, fewer observer ratings of exclusion by peers, teachers' reports of children's problem behavior, and peer nominations of aggression (Ladd & Proffitt, 1996). In the current study, internal consistency was strong ($\alpha = .76$). Parents rated girls as more empathic than boys, $t(189) = 2.20$, $p = .029$.

Observational assessment. Children's comforting behavior was assessed with a behavioral task previously used in a study of empathy (Zahn-Waxler, Robinson, & Emde, 1992). In the current study, children were presented with an opportunity to comfort a research assistant. Midway through the interview, research assistants "accidentally" shut the lid of a briefcase on their hand, then expressed pain with moderate vocalizations and pained facial expressions for 10 sec, after which the researchers lessened their expression of pain for 10–15 sec. Researchers avoided direct eye contact with their interviewees and noted whether the children attempted to comfort them or if they were unresponsive to their distress. Any empathic response including

TABLE 1

FACTOR ANALYSIS OF BRYAN'S INDEX OF EMPATHY FOR CHILDREN AND ADOLESCENTS (BIECA)

BIECA Item	Factor 1	Factor 2
Seeing a girl who is crying makes me feel like crying	**0.65**	−0.05
I get upset when I see a boy being hurt	**0.64**	0.19
Seeing a boy who is crying makes me feel like crying	**0.60**	0.07
It makes me sad to see a boy who can't find anyone to play with	**0.53**	0.29
I get upset when I see a girl being hurt	**0.52**	0.02
It makes me sad to see a girl who can't find anyone to play with	**0.51**	0.21
Some songs make me so sad I feel like crying	**0.44**	−0.08
Sometimes I cry when I watch TV	**0.41**	0.04
It's hard for me to see why someone else gets upset	**0.38**	−0.15
I get upset when I see an animal being hurt	**0.36**	0.03
Grown-ups sometimes cry, even when they have nothing to be sad about	**0.33**	−0.03
I get mad when I see a classmate pretending to need help from the teacher all the time	**0.31**	−0.10
Girls who cry because they are happy are silly	−0.07	**0.60**
Boys who cry because they are happy are silly	−0.09	**0.53**
People who kiss and hug in public are silly	−0.06	**0.51**
I think it is funny that some people cry during a sad movie or while reading a sad book	0.03	**0.50**
Kids who have no friends probably don't want any	0.05	**0.50**
I really like to watch people open presents, even when I don't get a present myself	0.21	**0.45**
It's silly to treat dogs and cats as though they have feelings like people	0.11	**0.34**
Eigenvalue	2.99	1.92
Variance accounted for (%)	13.61	8.72
Internal consistency	0.67	0.53

Note. BIECA = Bryant's Empathy Index for Children and Adolescents. Three items did not load on either factor and were deleted. Children respond to items with "Yes, this is like me" or "No, this is not like me." The correlation between Factor 1 and Factor 2 was .019, *ns*. Bold indicates which items load highest onto which factor.

behaviors/verbalizations such as asking "did that hurt?" and "are you OK?" offering tips to ease pain, or sharing stories about their own injuries were coded as comforting behaviors. Girls were more likely than boys to exhibit comforting behaviors, $\chi^2 = 7.41$, $p = .006$.

Research assistants were trained on administration of the observational task until consistency in procedures met study guidelines 100% of the time. At random intervals, research assistants' administration of the task with their participating child was observed to ensure that consistency in task administration was followed through the duration of data collection. Following data collection, using 25% of the protocols and based on the interviewers' field notes, inter-rater reliability regarding the presence or absence of empathic behavior was 100%.

Aggressive Behavior

Peer report. Given that peers are thought to provide the most valid evaluations of their classmates' aggressive behavior (Landau, Milich, & Whitten, 1994), a sociometric assessment was used to obtain this information (Hodges & Perry, 1999). A minimum classroom participation rate of 40% is recommended for sociometric measures (Terry & Cole, 1991) with classroom participation by grade in this study ranging from 54% to 69%. Children were presented with a list of participating classmates, excluding themselves. Using a 5-point scale (1 = not at all, 5 = a whole lot), children rated classmates on four aggressive behaviors including "this child hits/pushes/kicks," "this child starts fights," "this child is mean," and "this child gets mad easily." Scores for each item were generated by summing all peer ratings within a classroom and then dividing by the number of children who completed ratings. Because the four item ratings were highly correlated (r ranged from .78 to .87), item scores were summed to provide an overall aggression rating. There were no gender differences, $t(189) = 1.33$, $p = .19$.

RESULTS

Preliminary Analyses

Table 2 presents correlations between variables. Because child age, gender, and parent education and income were significantly associated with our measures of empathy, these variables were entered as covariates in the analyses that follow.

Of children with a currently incarcerated parent, the child's other parent or guardian completed the questionnaire packet. As the majority of currently incarcerated parents were fathers, these questionnaires were completed by children's mothers; in the two instances when a child's mother was currently incarcerated, these questionnaires were completed by the children's step-mother and grandmother. Of the 175 mothers who participated, 11 (6%) indicated that they had a history of incarceration. Of the nine fathers who participated, none indicated having experience with incarceration, two had experience with separation. Children who had experienced a past parental incarceration and were currently separated for other reasons were more likely to have a nonparental caregiver complete the questionnaires, $\chi^2 = 13.2$, $p = .02$ (28% compared to 13% in the CI group and CS-NoI groups, 8% in the NoS group, 4.5% in the PI group, and 0% in the PS-NoI group). Among the 18 nonparental guardians, only two reported a current parental incarceration and eight reported that the child had some experience with a past parental incarceration. There were no significant differences in children's self-, $F(6, 189) = 1.55$, $p = .165$, or parent-reported empathic behavior, $F(6, 180) = 1.89$, $p = .085$, rates of comforting, $\chi^2 = 4.14$, $p = .658$, or

TABLE 2

PEARSON PRODUCT MOMENT CORRELATIONS AMONG VARIABLES ASSESSED ($N = 210$ PARENT–CHILD DYADS)

	1	2	3	4	5	6	7	8	9	10	11	Mean (SD)
Child and family characteristics												
1. Child age	—	-.10	-.03	-.04	.01	.04	.02	.03	.05	.06	.13†	9.07 (1.10)
2. Child gender[a]		—	-.14*	.00	.26**	.16*	.19**	-.15*	-.02	-.15*	-.06	1.56 (0.49)
3. Parent education			—	.48**	-.01	.15*	-.07	-.09	-.10	-.09	-.09	3.99 (1.25)
4. Family income				—	.13†	.15*	-.05	-.24**	-.25**	-.23**	-.19**	3.69 (2.36)
Children's empathy												
5. Child-reported empathy					—	.21**	.26**	-.10	-.19*	-.11	-.10	7.57 (2.55)
6. Parent-reported child empathy						—	.12	-.34**	-.34**	-.32**	-.19**	14.02 (2.99)
7. Behavioral assessment[b]							—	-.12	-.09	-.05	-.06	0.39 (0.49)
Peer-rated aggressive behavior												
8. Peer-reports of "Hits"								—	.78**	.84**	.80**	1.75 (0.66)
9. Peer-reports of "Is mean"									—	.87**	.83**	1.85 (0.72)
10. Peer-reports of "Starts fights"										—	.83**	1.82 (0.73)
11. Peer-reports of "Gets mad a lot"											—	2.07 (0.82)

Note.
[a]Gender was coded as 1 = male, 2 = female. [b]Observational assessment of empathy was coded as 0 = did not comfort, 1 = comforted the researcher.
†$p < .10$. *$p < .05$. **$p < .01$.

peer-rated aggressive behavior, $F(6, 178) = 1.52$, $p = .175$ based on the caregiver's relation to the child.

Hypothesis 1: Group Differences Based on Experiences of Parental Separation and Incarceration

To examine differences among the six groups of children based on their experiences with parental separation and incarceration (the between subjects factor), we conducted a series of one-way ANCOVAs with children's gender, age, and parental education and income entered as covariates (see Table 3). Regarding parent-reported empathy, a significant main effect of Group was found, $F(5, 183) = 2.41$, $p = .038$, $\eta_p^2 = .065$. Follow-up post-hoc pairwise comparisons indicated that compared to the other groups of children, the CI children were rated by parents as being significantly less empathic than the following groups of children: NoS, $t(77) = 1.98$, $p = .015$; PS-NoI, $t(41) = 2.35$, $p = .015$; and PICS-NoI, $t(57) = 2.24$, $p = .005$. The CI group was marginally less empathic than the PI group, $t(45) = 1.65, p = .068$. There were no significant differences between the CI group and the CS-NoI group, $t(74) = 0.93$, $p = .205$.

A significant main effect for Group was found for the total peer-rated aggression variable, $F(5, 183) = 2.63$, $p = .026$, $\eta_p^2 = .072$. Post-hoc pairwise comparisons indicated that in comparison to the other groups, the CI children were rated by peers as being significantly more aggressive than the following groups of children: NoS, $t(77) = 2.60$, $p = .001$; PI, $t(45) = 1.96$, $p = .022$; and PS-NoI, $t(41) = 2.48$, $p = .007$. Marginally significant differences were found for the CS-NoI, $t(74) = 1.36$, $p = .059$; and the PICS-NoI, $t(57) = 1.29$, $p = .099$, groups of children, in which the CI group received higher aggression ratings.

Based on the ANCOVA analyses, there were no significant differences between the groups in children's self-reported empathy $F(5, 193) = 1.31$, $p = .262$, $\eta_p^2 = .035$, or on the empathy observational task, $F(5, 191) = 1.27$, $p = .277$, $\eta_p^2 = .034$.

Hypothesis 2: Unique Effect of a Current Parental Incarceration

To isolate the impact of a current parental incarceration on children's empathy and peer-rated aggression, hierarchical regression analyses were conducted using binary indicator variables to account for the experience of a past nonincarceration related separation (e.g., no past separation = 0, past separation = 1), experience of a past incarceration, experience of a current nonincarceration related separation, and experience of a current incarceration. This approach accounted for the multiple and varied types of separations children experienced in our sample. The binary variable

17

TABLE 3

DESCRIPTIVE DATA ON CHILDREN'S PROSOCIAL EMPATHIC BEHAVIOR AND PEER-RATED AGGRESSIVE BEHAVIOR BY CHILDREN'S CURRENT AND PAST EXPERIENCES WITH SEPARATION FROM PARENTS FOR REASONS RELATED TO INCARCERATION AND OTHER REASONS

Children's experience with separation and incarceration[a]	NoS (n = 54)	PS-NoI (n = 18)	CS-NoI (n = 51)	PI (n = 22)	CI (n = 24)	PICS-NoI (n = 34)
Self-reported empathy	8.07 (2.21)	7.57 (2.91)	7.44 (2.47)	6.55 (2.82)	7.29 (2.79)	7.84 (2.56)
Parent-reported empathy	14.74 (2.61)	14.63 (2.45)	13.48 (3.33)	13.95 (3.41)	12.38 (2.69)	14.71 (2.71)
Proportion of children who comforted	0.43 (0.50)	0.50 (0.51)	0.35 (0.48)	.036 (0.49)	0.21 (0.41)	0.50 (0.51)
Peer-rated aggression						
Hits	1.51 (0.53)	1.57 (0.61)	1.83 (0.66)	1.71 (0.57)	2.27 (0.77)	1.95 (0.70)
Is mean	1.63 (0.64)	1.54 (0.60)	1.95 (0.67)	1.81 (0.66)	2.25 (0.89)	2.08 (0.78)
Gets mad a lot	1.82 (0.70)	1.81 (0.89)	2.24 (0.84)	2.03 (0.64)	2.50 (0.97)	2.28 (0.83)
Starts fights	1.58 (0.63)	1.61 (0.74)	1.89 (0.62)	1.76 (0.66)	2.37 (0.96)	2.02 (0.78)
Total peer-rated aggression[b]	6.39 (2.30)	6.63 (2.66)	7.89 (2.55)	7.32 (2.28)	9.38 (3.43)	8.30 (2.80)

Note.
[a]NoS, children have never been separated from parents; PS-NoI, children who have experienced a past separation from parents for reasons other than incarceration; CS-NoI, children who are experiencing a current separation for reasons other than incarceration; PI, children have experienced a past parental incarceration; CI, children who are experiencing a current parental incarceration; PICS-NoI, children who have experienced a past parental incarceration and are currently separated from a parent for reasons other than incarceration.
[b]Total peer-rated aggression is the sum of the four peer-rated sociometric behaviors.

indicating a current parental incarceration was entered last in the last step of the regression analyses.

Controlling for child age and gender, parent education, and family income, the amount of unique variance that a current parental incarceration accounted for in the prediction of children's empathy and peer-rated aggressive behavior was examined (see Table 4). Over and above the influence of demographic variables, past separation and incarceration experiences, and current separation for nonincarceration reasons, a current parental incarceration accounted for unique variance in the prediction of parent-reported empathy ($\Delta R^2 = .02$, $p = .038$, $f^2 = .11$), and peer-rated aggressive behavior ($\Delta R^2 = .06$, $p = .001$, $f^2 = .09$). It did not add significantly to the prediction of child-reported empathy, ($\Delta R^2 = .00$, ns) or observed comforting/empathy ($\Delta R^2 = .01$, ns).

Hypothesis 3: Empathy as a Protective Factor

To examine the moderating impact of children's empathy, we created interaction terms by mean centering the binary current parental incarceration variable and then multiplying it by the mean centered empathy variables (child self-report, parent-report, observed empathy). Hierarchical regression analyses with the interaction variable entered in the final step were then conducted (see Table 5). The results indicated that the interaction between child-reported empathy and the experience of a current parental incarceration significantly predicted children's peer-reported aggressive behavior; the effect size of this interaction term is moderate, $f^2 = .18$. Children's empathic responding moderated the relation between a current parental incarceration and children's aggressive behavior (see Figure 1). Specifically, when children reported high levels of empathy, they were not at increased risk of aggressive peer relations, even if they were experiencing a current parental incarceration. Post-hoc testing indicated that in the CI group of children, self-reported empathy was a significant predictor of peer-rated aggressive behavior, $\beta = -.50$, $\Delta R^2 = .203$, $p = .053$, whereas self-reported empathy was not a significant predictor of peer-rated aggression for children not experiencing a current parental incarceration, $\beta = -.07$, $\Delta R^2 = .005$, $p = .372$. Parent-reported child empathy and our observations of empathy did not moderate the relation between CI and peer-rated aggression (see Table 5).

DISCUSSION

Research has demonstrated that children with an incarcerated parent are at increased risk for a number of problematic outcomes, yet few studies have examined protective factors that may moderate the impact of a parental

TABLE 4

REGRESSION ANALYSES PREDICTING CHILDREN'S EMPATHY AND PEER-RATED AGGRESSIVE BEHAVIORS BY EXPERIENCES WITH CURRENT AND PAST PARENTAL SEPARATION AND INCARCERATION

	Self-Reported Empathy		Parent-Reported Empathy		Observations of Comforting Behavior		Peer-Rated Aggression[a]	
	B (SE) β	ΔR^2	B (SE) β	ΔR^2	B (SE) β	ΔR^2	B (SE) β	ΔR^2
Step 1: Demographic variables		.10**		.07*		.05†		.07*
Child age	-0.02 (.14)	-.00	0.30 (.20)	.11	.02 (.03)	.05	-0.01 (.20)	-.00
Child gender[b]	1.52 (.37)	.30**	1.05 (.44)	.17*	.02 (.07)	.21**	-0.40 (.41)	-.07
Parent education	-0.04 (.17)	-.02	0.30 (.19)	.13	-.01 (.03)	-.01	-0.06 (.20)	-.03
Family income	0.18 (.09)	.17*	0.07 (.11)	.06	-.01 (.02)	-.05	-0.12 (.11)	-.09
Step 2: Other incarceration and separation experiences[c]		.01		.03		.02		.01
Experienced a past parental separation (nonincarceration)	-0.20 (.68)	-.02	0.68 (.82)	.07	.11 (.14)	.06†	0.02 (.72)	.00
Experienced a past parental incarceration	-0.12 (.45)	-.02	0.67 (.54)	.10	.09 (.09)	.08	0.32 (.48)	.05
Experiencing a current parental separation (nonincarceration)	0.42 (.45)	.08	-0.45 (.54)	-.07	.00 (.09)	.00	1.03 (.05)	.19*
Step 3: Experience of current incarceration[d]		.00		.02*		.01		.06*
Experiencing a current parental incarceration	0.13 (.65)	.02	-1.62 (.77)	-.18*	-.16 (.13)	-.11	2.48 (.74)	.28*

Note.
[a] Peer-rated aggression is a sum of the four peer-rated sociometric behaviors (e.g., This child "Hits," "Is Mean," "Starts Fights," and "Gets Mad A Lot").
[b] Child Gender was coded as 1 = male, 2 = female.
[c] Each of these were coded as binary indicator variables.
[d] This was coded as a binary indicator variable. All data are from the last step of the regression model.
† $p < .10$. * $p < .05$. ** $p < .01$.

TABLE 5

Regression Analyses Predicting Children's Peer-Rated Aggressive Behaviors[a] by Interaction of Current Incarceration With Empathic Reports and Observation

	Empathy Variables								
	Child Self-report			Parent-Report			Observed Comforting		
	B (SE)	β	ΔR²	B (SE)	β	ΔR²	B (SE)	β	ΔR²
Step 1: Demographic variables			.07*			.08**			.07**
Child age	-0.03 (.19)	-.01		0.11 (.19)	.04		-0.01 (.20)	-.01	
Child gender[b]	-0.22 (.42)	-.04		0.11 (.39)	.01		-0.36 (.42)	-.07	
Parent education	-0.02 (.18)	-.01		0.02 (.17)	.00		-0.06 (.18)	-.02	
Family income	-0.13 (.10)	-.11		-0.13 (.10)	-.11		-0.14 (.11)	-.12	
Step 2: Other incarceration and separation experiences			.01			.01			.01
Experienced a past parental separation (nonincarceration)	0.09 (.72)	.01		0.46 (.69)	.05		-0.08 (.75)	-.01	
Experienced a past parental incarceration	0.43 (.48)	.07		0.62 (.46)	.10		0.27 (.49)	.04	
Experiencing a current parental separation (nonincarceration)	1.17 (.48)	.02*		1.08 (.46)	.19*		1.06 (.49)	.19*	
Step 3: Experience of current incarceration			.06**			.07**			.05**
Experiencing a current parental incarceration[d]	2.45 (.74)	.28**		1.78 (.71)	.26**		2.23 (.84)	.25**	
Step 4: Empathy			.01			.07**			.00
Empathy variable[c]	-0.10 (.08)	-.10		-0.25 (.07)	-.29**		-0.25 (.44)	-.03	
Step 5: Interaction term[d]			.02*			.01			.00
Current incarceration X empathy	-0.35 (.18)	-.14*		-0.25 (.21)	-.10		-0.12 (.27)	-.04	

Note

[a] Peer-rated children's aggressive behaviors is a sum of the four peer-rated sociometric behaviors (e.g., This child "Hits," "Is Mean," "Starts Fights," and "Gets Mad A Lot").

[b] Child Gender was coded as 1 = male, 2 = female.

[c] The empathy variable was either the child self-report, the parent-report, or the observed comforting variable.

[d] The interaction term was created by mean centering the incarceration is current variable and each of the empathy variables and then multiplying them; this interaction term was entered in the final step and all presented regression weights were obtained from the final step of each model.

* p < .05. ** p < .01.

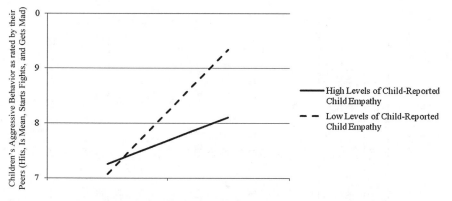

FIGURE 1.—Interaction between a parent's current incarceration and children's self-reported empathy on children's peer-rated aggressive behaviors.

incarceration on children's social psychosocial adjustment. The current study examined children's empathy as a protective factor in children with incarcerated parents and found evidence that in the context of the highly stressful, multifaceted risk of parental incarceration, children's self-reported empathy served as a protective factor against aggressive peer relations. Specifically, although children who were experiencing a parental incarceration were more likely to be rated as aggressive by peers, when these children reported high levels of empathy, they were no more likely to be rated as aggressive than their classmates who had not experienced parental incarceration. These results held even when controlling for demographic variables and previous parental incarceration and separations.

Another intriguing finding indicated that, relative to classmates, some of whom experienced a past parental incarceration, children experiencing a current parental incarceration evidenced fewer parent/guardian-reported empathic behaviors. These results support our proposition that there may be a depletion of emotional resources within the family unit during a current parental incarceration that reduces children's motivation and skills to reach out to others in prosocial, empathic ways. This seeming lack of empathy may then facilitate their aggressive responses to their peers.

There may be unique effects of separation from parents on children's empathy, as there were no significant differences in parent-reported empathy between children experiencing current parental incarceration and children currently separated from parents for reasons other than incarceration. This finding underscores the importance of delineating the processes and adaptations families make in response to a parent's incarceration. Future research should address the need to more fully understand how children's attachment system is impacted by stressful separation experiences especially given that some researchers have proposed that parental incarceration undermines children's sense of security and may disrupt and disorganize children's attachment representations (e.g., Parke & Clarke-Stewart, 2001; Poehlmann, 2005a). In turn, these disruptions could influence the expression of empathy, since it is thought to develop from within a secure attachment relationship (e.g., Grusec & Davido, 2010).

Of note, no group differences were found in children's self-reported empathy or empathy as observed in a behavioral task, suggesting that the set of empathy findings appear to be sensitive to measurement issues. Specifically, there were significant differences between groups on peer-rated aggressive behavior and parent-rated empathy. However, the parent-reported empathy measure largely reflected parents' observations of children behaving in prosocial ways with peers and overlaps conceptually with empathy as well as peer relations. Because there were group differences for both of these measures, it is likely that children's peer relations are negatively impacted by a current parental incarceration. However, given the lack of significant group differences in self-reported empathy and empathic responding to the research assistant, empathy may not be directly impacted by a current parental incarceration, but, rather, is a moderator of the relations between a current incarceration and aggressive peer relations.

The current study expands upon and replicates knowledge of how children cope with parental incarceration. First, because children were recruited from a school-based sample that provided variability in family contexts, we were able to examine differences among children who had never been separated from parents, children who were separated from parents for reasons other than incarceration, and differences between children experiencing past and current parental incarceration. Much of the previous research has examined children with an incarcerated parent and not included a relevant comparison group (Hagen et al., 2005; Poehlmann, 2005a) or has examined differences among children with or without a family history of incarceration or involvement with the criminal justice system (e.g., Phillips et al., 2004). By having multiple groups of children with varying levels of separation and incarceration experiences, we were better able to isolate the unique effect of a current incarceration on children's adjustment.

Second, this research included several methodological improvements such as the use of a multireporter (child, parent, peer) and multimethod approach that included questionnaires as well as behavioral tasks. We chose to ask children about their empathy because research indicates that children are the best reporters of their emotions, including empathy, and internal experiences given their access to these experiences that are not always shared publicly (Achenbach, McConaughy, & Howell, 1987; Durbin, 2010). The use of peer ratings of aggressive behavior is a particular strength as peers offer a unique and invaluable perspective on children's social functioning (Rubin, Bukowski, & Parker, 1998). Further, parent/guardian- and child-reported empathy were also significantly correlated suggesting a notable concordance in perceptions, which is often not found when examining parent–child agreement on emotion regulation variables (Hourigan, Goodman, & Southam-Gerow, 2011). Finally, our observational index of empathic responding was positively correlated with child self-report of empathy, providing a degree of confidence in the validity of the results and adding a new methodological perspective to this area of inquiry.

Despite the study's contributions, its limitations suggest several avenues for future research. First, greater attention to parent and child gender differences is warranted. With a larger sample size, we could have examined the role that child and parent gender may play in children's responses to parental incarceration and separation. Second, more in-depth examination of the specific experiences related to a parental incarceration is needed because, for instance, the type and frequency of contact children have with their incarcerated parent may impact children's adjustment and peer relations during a parent's incarceration (Poehlmann et al., 2010). Moreover, it is important to document the type of corrections facility (e.g., jail vs. prison), the nature of the parent's crime, and the length of the parent's sentence in future research, as these variables may contribute to children's experience of parental incarceration. Finally, future studies should examine additional protective factors such as attachment security. Although we framed this study from an attachment perspective, we did not assess attachment relationships. In future research, a reliable, valid measure of attachment representations or relationships for school-age children should be incorporated (see Kerns & Richardson, 2005). Emotion regulation skills are another potentially key protective factor that needs future empirical attention and is explored further in the second study summarized in this volume.

The results of the current study can be used to inform preventive interventions for children, parents, and families impacted by parental incarceration. It is possible that increasing children's empathic responding may help reduce problematic peer relations or peer-directed aggression in children of incarcerated parents. School-based interventions that promote empathic responding, such as the Child Development Project (Solomon, Battistich, Watson, & Schaps, 2000), the Roots of Empathy project (Schonert-Reichl & Scott, 2009), or the PATHs program (Izard et al., 2008), might be worthwhile to consider in areas that have a high proportion of children affected by parental incarceration. These interventions are evidence-based, with demonstrated efficacy in increasing children's empathy. Such an intervention effort at the school-level would have the additional benefit of helping children with incarcerated parents, while not singling these children out, a criticism of other school-based efforts that are designed only for children of incarcerated parents (see Lopez & Bhat, 2007). Future research should explore efficacy of these programs with children of incarcerated parents.

Children with incarcerated parents face numerous risks in their environments and often struggle at school with teachers and peers. It is encouraging that the results of the current study suggest that when these children feel empathic toward others, their risk for problematic, aggressive peer relations significantly decreases. More research is needed on additional protective factors in this population that may help foster resilience processes in this growing population of children and youth.

III. TEASING, BULLYING, AND EMOTION REGULATION IN CHILDREN OF INCARCERATED MOTHERS

Barbara J. Myers, Virginia H. Mackintosh, Maria I. Kuznetsova, Geri M. Lotze, Al M. Best, and Neeraja Ravindran

Jason teases his fellow camper, Dwayne, daring him into the deep end of the pool, knowing that Dwayne cannot swim. What was Jason's intention with this tease? Is Jason cementing their friendship with a friendly gibe, or is he trying to belittle with a deliberate insult? And how does Dwayne interpret the tease? Will he laugh it off ("Nah, I think I'll pass on drowning today"), or pummel Jason to the ground, believing he has been bullied? For the teaser and the teased, there is an intention and an interpretation to teasing.

For better or for worse, every child, adolescent, and adult is teased; it is a normative part of living (Warm, 1997). Teasing can be playful or hurtful, but the line between the two is not always clear (Keltner, Capps, Kring, Young, & Heerey, 2001). The ambiguity between hostile and friendly teasing is part of the very nature of teasing, and teasing can cross into bullying (Mills & Carwile, 2009). Whereas teasing may be positive, bullying is always negative, as it intentionally inflicts injury or discomfort upon another (Olweus, 2006). Teasing is universal, but there is tremendous variability in how well children cope with teasing and the extent to which their own gibes are designed to hurt others. Although some topics allow for lighthearted joking, having a parent in prison is a tender subject for children and is an easy target for cruel teasing. Furthermore, we know that children who report feeling high levels of stigma around their mothers' incarceration tend to act out aggressively (Hagen & Myers, 2003). Their aggressive behavior can include bullying their peers.

In contrast, many children of incarcerated parents exhibit positive behavior and adjustment (Nesmith & Ruhland, 2008), and we need to know more about the processes that facilitate such resilience. We propose that children's prosocial teasing, prosocial behavior with peers, and avoidance of

Corresponding author: Barbara J. Myers, 808 W. Franklin Street, Virginia Commonwealth University, Richmond VA 23284-2018, email: bmyers@vcu.edu

bullying result, in part, from children's ability to regulate their emotions. Thus, a child's emotion regulation may serve as a protective factor against engaging in bullying behavior. In this study, we sought to find how bullying behavior in children of incarcerated mothers was predicted by dual aspects (i. e., both the positive and the negative sides) of teasing, peer interaction, and emotion regulation. Exhibiting resilience is both difficult and critical for children whose families are affected by incarceration (Nesmith & Ruhland, 2008). A child's capacity to regulate emotions—and to manage bullying and teasing—may relate to their overall competence, potentially facilitating resilience (Shields & Cicchetti, 2001).

Teasing Can Be Hostile or Friendly

Three components of teasing—aggression, humor, and ambiguity—are at the heart of what makes teasing both dangerous and attractive (Shapiro, Baumeister, & Kessler, 1991). As Warm (1997) explained, "[Teasing] is a source of universal suffering as well as a means of expressing power, sadism and friendly humor" (p. 97). When asked, children more often see teasing as aggressive rather than fun. When third, fifth, and eighth grade children wrote compositions about teasing, they talked about name calling and making fun of the attributes of others, and they said the usual targets of teasing were smaller children, "losers," and "stupid" children (Shapiro et al., 1991). Similarly, Warm (1997) analyzed written responses to questions about teasing from 250 children in the 1st grade through 11th grade. An average of 80% of students' reasons for teasing involved aggressive intent that included pleasure in the misery of the victim, revenge, and drive for power. Warm observed that the dominant motivation for children's teasing seemed at every age to be "sadistic pleasure in the discomfort of the child being teased" (p. 97), and Scambler, Harris, & Milich (1998) observe that the message to the recipient is most often hostile and is likely to consist of taunting, verbal abuse, and insults.

Barnett, Burns, Sanborn, Bartel, and Wilds (2004) found a more positive view of childhood teasing, however, in their study with fifth and sixth grade children. They offer an example of a prosocial tease: Two friends are in gym class, and one boy teases the other that his feet are growing so big that, "you'll have to borrow shoes from some giant NBA superstar like Shaquille O'Neal" (p. 295). In this type of teasing, the "target" child is actually pleased, as the teaser is joking and having a good time with the one being kidded. Both teachers and peers rated children as showing a greater tendency to be prosocial teasers than antisocial teasers. Voss (1997) similarly demonstrated that in the early school years, children use teasing to express liking for each other, while Eder (1991) found that adolescent group members tease each other to increase cohesion and solidify group membership.

Children need both emotional and cognitive skills to understand the subtleties of teasing. As a recipient of teases, the child needs to interpret whether the instigator had a friendly or a hostile intention, an ability that relies on understanding that an act can have multiple, contradictory intentions. A child then needs to have the emotional ability to react appropriately. Children who report negative experiences and attitudes about being teased interpret ambiguous teases as if they were meant to be hostile and antisocial. These same children tend to use ineffective coping mechanisms in response to ambiguous teasing. They reported that they would retaliate, physically and verbally, or tell the teacher (Barnett, Barlett, Livengood, Murphy, & Brewton, 2010). This hostile attribution bias, along with an immature response, could set them up for further alienation and rejection from their peers (Crick & Dodge, 1994; Dodge et al., 2003).

Bullying

Like teasing, childhood bullying occurs frequently. In a nationwide study of 15,686 students in grades 6 through 10, 29% of the students reported having been involved in some aspect of bullying, either as a bully, a victim, or both (National Institute of Child Health and Human Development, 2001). Unlike teasing, which may be playful, bullying always has a hostile intent. As defined by Olweus (1993, p. 10), a child "is being bullied or victimized when he/she is exposed repeatedly and over time to negative action on the part of one or more other students." "Negative action" can be anything that provides discomfort and upsets the targeted child, from verbal put-downs to physical attacks to exclusion from a group. Bullying is intentional, not an accident, and it happens in an interpersonal relationship characterized by an imbalance of power (Olweus, 2006).

To an observer, the distinction between teasing and bullying is not always clear, however, particularly during middle childhood. Verbal aggression during this stage replaces the more physical aggression seen in preschoolers, so there are more snide remarks than punches (Warm, 1997). Since the intent behind teasing is often subtle, an outside observer, unable to know the motivations behind a remark, can only assess the distinction between teasing and bullying by seeing "how participants are presenting, and responding to, the teasing comments" (Mills & Carwile, 2009, p. 282). Still, a child's status as a bully is clear to both adults and children (Shields & Cicchetti, 2001). School systems show their disapproval of teasing by incorporating interventions programs designed to stop both teasing and bullying (Mills & Carwile, 2009).

Emotion Regulation

Emotion regulation is the "ability to manage one's subjective experience of emotion, especially its intensity and duration, and to manage strategically one's expression of emotion in communicative contexts" (Saarni, 1999, p. 220). It requires emotional competence to interpret the level of hostility— or playful fun—inherent in a tease and to choose to respond appropriately.

While children may know intellectually that humor is the most effective reaction to teasing (Scambler et al., 1998), they may not have the ability to refrain from an emotionally dysregulated reaction such as anger or tears.

Children of incarcerated mothers are at especially high risk for emotion dysregulation. In earlier work with children of incarcerated mothers, a worrisome number of children showed problems in both the positive and the negative aspects of emotion regulation, and poor emotion regulation was related to heightened externalizing, internalizing, and callous-unemotional traits (Lotze et al., 2010). The development of emotion regulation is not simply a matter of maturation but is learned through interaction with others, especially within the family (Eisenberg, Cumberland, & Spinrad, 1998; Morris, Silk, Steinberg, Myers, & Robinson, 2007; Saarni, Mumme, & Campos, 1998). Negative parenting (e.g., hostility, negative control, lack of sensitivity) is associated with poor emotion regulation in children (Calkins, Smith, Gill, & Johnson, 1998; Morris et al., 2007). While the quality of parenting and home life for children of incarcerated parents varies tremendously (Dallaire, 2007a; Mackintosh et al., 2006), for some it may threaten their emotion regulation. Chaotic households can make it difficult for children to anticipate events and be planful, thus ending up emotionally labile (Evans, Gonnella, Marcynyszyn, Gentile, & Salpekar, 2005).

Along with family influences, children have their own temperamental qualities that influence their emotion regulation. Children predisposed toward high negative reactivity experience higher levels of anger, frustration, and irritability, and these children are at risk for behavioral and emotional problems (Morris et al., 2007), especially when parental guidance is poor or lacking. The relationship between emotional negativity/lability and quality of parenting is dynamic, in that difficult children are more likely to evoke negative responses from their caregivers (Bell, 1968; Sameroff, 2000). Children who are maltreated show dysregulated emotions (either over-controlled or undercontrolled) in the face of simulated anger (Maughan & Cicchetti, 2002). The quality of caregiving is thus critical in assisting children who are already at risk for problems managing their emotions.

Peer relationships also shape, and are shaped by, emotion regulation. As children move into middle childhood, more and more of the feedback regarding the display of emotions comes from peers (Kopp, 1989). Social competence requires the increasing internalization and use of these messages as to norms of behavior that are appropriate to the context (Denham, 1998). Peers provide constant feedback as to what behaviors are acceptable or not, and children who are unable to manage their emotions within the established boundaries are often rejected (Rose-Krasnor, 1997). Therefore, poor regulation of emotions is linked to problems with peer acceptance (Shields & Cicchetti, 2001). This relationship is dynamic, as those children who are not accepted make attractive targets for hostile teasing, and those who respond inappropriately to teasing risk further rejection by their peers.

Both bullies and victims show deficits in emotion regulation. Shields and Cicchetti (2001) investigated emotion dysregulation as a predictor of bullying and victimization in maltreated and nonmaltreated children age 8–12 years at a summer camp. Emotion dysregulation was correlated with both disruptive and withdrawn behaviors. More specifically, disruptive behaviors were associated with bullying, whereas withdrawal-submissiveness was associated with victimization. Both bullies and victims were more emotionally dysregulated than other children. Moreover, there are long-term consequences to poor emotion regulation. Problems with modulation and expression of emotions are linked to both externalizing and internalizing behaviors, difficulties in relationships with caregivers, and poor peer relationships (Denham, 1998; Eisenberg et al., 2001).

Purpose and Hypotheses

This study was designed to explore potential mechanisms to explain bullying in children of incarcerated mothers. In line with resilience research, we asserted that there are desirable factors that help attenuate bullying as well as negative factors related to more bullying. We proposed that bullying would be predicted by the dual aspects of teasing, peer interaction, and emotion regulation. More specifically, we hypothesized that membership in a high bully group would be related to more hostile teasing (and less playful teasing), more aggressive behavior with peers (and less prosocial behavior with peers), and more negative emotion regulation (and less positive emotion regulation). We used independent measures to assess the two aspects of each of these predictors.

METHOD

Participants

Participants were 61 children (55.7% girls), 7–13 years ($M = 9.7$, $SD = 1.6$), attending a 6-day, sleepover summer camp for children of incarcerated mothers. Children self-identified as African American (67.2%), mixed race (16.4%), European American (13.1%), and Hispanic (3.3%). All were children of currently or formerly incarcerated mothers; by camp policy, children whose mothers were now released from jail or prison were welcome to attend camp and take part in research. Children were currently living with grandparents (39.3%; including grandmother alone, 16.4%, or both grandparents, 23%), mother (29.5%; including mother alone, 18%; mother and father, 8.2%; or mother and other, 3.3%), father (13.1%), aunt (8.2%), or other (relative, friend; 9.8%). Additional background data about mothers and families were not available. While at camp, children were assigned a same-sex mentor, with whom they spent the entire 6 days. Each mentor was assigned a maximum of two campers, with most mentor/camper matches being one-on-one.

Measures

Adult Rating of Antisocial and Prosocial Teasing (Barnett et al., 2004)

Adopted from Barnett, this is a rating (1–5, *never* to *all the time*) of an adult's rating of the child as an antisocial teaser and prosocial teaser. The measure provided the following definitions:

Type 1 Teases are mean teasing. They purposely hurt another person's feelings; the person who is teased ends up feeling sad or hurt.

Type 2 Teases are playful and fun teasing. The person who is teased thinks it is funny and feels happy about being kidded. Nobody feels hurt or mad afterward.

Mentors rated children in three contexts at camp: during daytime camp activities and moving between activities; while in the cabin with the other kids; and during evening camp activities. A sample question is, *How often does this child do Type 1 (hurtful) teasing while in the cabin with the other kids?* Internal reliability (Cronbach's alpha) for antisocial teasing was .95 and for prosocial teasing was .91. Higher mean scores indicate higher levels of each kind of teasing.

Child Behavior Scale (CBS; Ladd & Proffitt, 1996)

The CBS is an adult-report measure of children's aggressive, prosocial, and withdrawn behaviors in interaction with peers. The full scale has six subscales, of which two were employed here: Aggressive with Peers (sample, "kicks, bites, hits") and Prosocial with Peers (sample, "kind toward peers"). Items are rated on a three-point response scale, $1 = doesn't apply$, $2 = applies$ *sometimes*, and $3 = certainly$ *applies*. Internal reliabilities were $\alpha = .92$ for Aggressive with Peers and $\alpha = .92$ for Prosocial with Peers. Higher mean scores indicate higher levels of each subscale.

Emotion Regulation Checklist (ERC; Shields & Cicchetti, 1997)

The ERC is an adult-report measure of a child's emotion regulation. Its authors used the measure with low-income, primarily minority status children ages 6–12, in a summer camp. The 24 items make up two subscales. The Lability/Negativity subscale is a measure of poor emotion regulation that assesses arousal, reactivity, anger dysregulation, and mood lability. A sample item is *Responds angrily to limit-setting by adults*. The Emotion Regulation subscale evaluates empathy, appropriate emotional expression, and emotional selfawareness; a sample item is *Responds positively to neutral or friendly overtures from peers*. Internal consistency reliability with this sample was .92 for Lability/Negativity and .71 for Emotion Regulation. High scores on Lability/Negativity indicate poor emotion regulation; high scores on the Emotion Regulation subscale indicate better emotion regulation.

Mount Hope Bully-Victim Questionnaire (Shields & Cicchetti, 2001)

This eight-item adult-report questionnaire measures children's bullying behavior and vulnerability to victimization. Only the five-item bullying subscale was used here, and Cronbach's α was .93. It was first developed for use by counselors in a summer camp setting for inner-city low-income children and so is particularly appropriate for the present study. Using a four-point Likert-type scale (never, seldom, sometimes, often), camp counselors/mentors rate how frequently children display bullying behavior. The measure permits researchers to classify children as high/low bullies. Shields & Cicchetti (2001) classified children as bullies who scored at least one standard deviation above the mean on the bully subscale and below one standard deviation above the mean on the victim subscale. The sample size in the current study was too small to form a meaningful bully group in this way (i.e., the bully group would have had just 10 children). Thus, High and Low bully groups were formed by splitting the variable at its mean (1.87, *seldom*), so that High bullies scored above and Low bullies below a score of 1.87.

Procedure

Children were attending a summer camp conducted by a faith-based organization for children of incarcerated mothers. This 6-day sleepover camp included typical camp activities (e.g., swimming, arts and crafts, nature hikes) and was provided at no cost to families. Our research group has been part of the camp since its inception. Information about the study was mailed to registering families as part of the precamp information packet. Consent forms were included in the packet and were signed by the primary caregivers and brought to camp by the children. Only the children with signed consents were evaluated by their mentors.

The measures were completed by camp mentors, who were adult volunteers (college students and members of the faith group) who supervised and camped with the children all week. Mentors participated in a training period prior to camp during which the researchers explained the study, including the behaviors that were to be measured. Mentors signed consents. Mentors came to know their children well in both structured and unstructured contexts, as they were with the children 24 hr a day for 6 days (see Pellegrini & Bartini, 2000; Shields & Cicchetti, 2001, for discussion of adults' ability to rate aggression and bullying in children with whom they work). At the end of the week, mentors completed questionnaires for their assigned children. No compensation was provided for taking part in the study. The study was approved by the University Institutional Review Board (IRB).

RESULTS

Table 6 shows adults' ratings of antisocial and prosocial teasing and subscales of the CBS, the ERC, and the Mount Hope Bully-Victim Questionnaire. We hypothesized that membership in the high bullying group would be predicted by higher antisocial teasing, lower prosocial teasing, higher Aggression with Peers of the CBS, lower Prosocial with Peers of the CBS, higher Lability/Negativity of the ERC, and lower Emotion Regulation of the ERC. Sample size was not sufficient to include all the predictors in one model.

Logistic regression allows one to predict a discrete outcome such as group membership (here, High/Low bully groups) from a set of variables that may be continuous, discrete, dichotomous, or a mix (Tabachnik & Fidell, 2007). Logistic regression also lends itself to a clear interpretation of the probability of bullying as a function of the predictors. A hierarchical logistic regression model was built using antisocial teasing as a predictor of membership in High/Low bullying group and adjusting for age and gender (see Model 1 in

TABLE 6

ADULT MENTORS' REPORTS OF CHILDREN'S BEHAVIORS

Measure	Boys ($n = 26$)		Girls ($n = 35$)		All ($N = 61$)	
	Mean	SD	Mean	SD	Mean	SD
Adult rating of antisocial and prosocial teasing						
Antisocial teasing	2.56	1.20	1.75	.78	2.10	1.05
Prosocial teasing	2.29	0.77	2.49	.89	2.40	0.84
Child behavior scale						
Aggressive with peers	1.90	0.67	1.43	.43	1.63	0.59
Prosocial with peers	1.89	0.51	2.36	.55	2.16	0.58
Emotion regulation checklist						
Lability/negativity subscale	2.39	0.77	1.98	.57	2.16	0.69
Emotion regulation subscale	2.94	0.55	3.16	.48	3.06	0.52
Mount hope bully-victim questionnaire						
Bullying	2.28	1.02	1.57	.71	1.87	0.92

Table 7). A test of the full model, including antisocial teasing, was statistically significant [$X^2(3) = 27.21$, $p < .001$]. With all three variables included in the model, 84% of cases were correctly predicted; 92% of Low bullies and 72% of High bullies were correctly predicted. Gender of the child was a significant predictor of bullying group [$X^2(1) = 4.26$, $p = .04$], with boys higher, but age not significant [$X^2(1) = .002$, $p = .97$]. Age was not a significant predictor in any of the models shown in Table 2. Antisocial teasing was a significant predictor of bullying group [$X^2(1) = 10.51$, $p = .001$] when adjusted for age and gender. The change in odds associated with a one-unit change in antisocial teasing was 4.3, indicating that a one-unit change in antisocial teasing behavior resulted in a child being more than four times more likely to be a High bully. A test of a similar model using prosocial teasing was not significant. Prosocial teasing was not a predictor of bully group.

A similar model with the Aggressive with Peers subscale of the CBS was also tested (see Model 2 in Table 7). A test of the full model was found

TABLE 7

HIERARCHICAL LOGISTIC REGRESSION MODELS PREDICTING CHILDREN'S HIGH/LOW BULLYING GROUPS FROM ADULT MENTORS' PREDICTORS

Prediction of High/Low Bullying	Chi-Square	Percent Predicted Correctly (%)	95% CI for Odds Ratio (OR)	Adjusted OR
Model 1	27.21**	83.6		
Gender			1.07–15.02	4.01*
Age			0.67–1.46	0.99
Antisocial teasing			1.78–10.32	4.28**
Model 2	37.84**	80.3		
Gender			.89–19.15	4.14
Age			0.75–1.82	1.17
Aggressive with peers (CBS)			5.89–282	40.77**
Model 3	21.27**	78.7		
Gender			1.08–13.52	3.83*
Age			0.74–1.53	1.06
Prosocial with peers (CBS)			0.05–0.57	0.17*
Model 4	33.96**	83.3		
Gender			1.45–30.75	6.68*
Age			0.65–1.52	0.99
Lability/Negativity (ERC)			3.7–100	19.27**
Model 5	18.53**	71.7		
Gender			1.6–18.52	5.44*
Age			0.67–1.41	0.97
Emotion Regulation (ERC)			0.43–0.7	0.17*

Note. CBS = Child Behavior Scale; ERC = Emotion Regulation Checklist.
*$p < .05$, **$p < .001$.

statistically significant $[X^2(3) = 37.84, p < .001]$, and with all three variables included in the model, 80% of cases were correctly predicted; 89% of Low bullies; and 68% of High bullies were correctly predicted. The Aggressive with Peers subscale of the CBS was a significant predictor of bullying group $[X^2(1) = 14.12, p < .001]$ when adjusted for age and gender. The change in odds associated with a one-unit change in aggression with peers was 40.8, indicating that a one-unit change in aggressive behavior with peers resulted in a participant being 41 times more likely to be a High bully, when adjusting for age and gender.

An additional model was tested with the Prosocial with Peers subscale of the CBS entered in the model (see Model 3 in Table 7). The full model was found to be statistically significant $[X^2(3) = 21.27, p < .001]$. With all three variables included in the model, 79% of cases were correctly predicted; 83% of Low bullies; and 72% of High bullies were correctly predicted. Prosocial behavior with peers as measured by the CBS was a significant predictor of high bullying behavior $[X^2(1) = 8.11, p = .004]$ when adjusted for age and gender. The change in odds associated with a one-unit change in Emotion Regulation was .17, indicating that a one-unit change in prosocial behavior score resulted in a participant being 5.9 times *less* likely to be a High bully.

A similar model with the Lability/Negativity score of the ERC was also tested (Model 4, Table 7). The full model was found to be statistically significant $[X^2(3) = 33.96, p < .001]$, and 83% of cases were correctly predicted; 89% of Low bullies; and 76% of High bullies were correctly predicted. Lability/Negativity was a significant predictor of bullying group $[X^2(1) = 12.35, p < .001]$ when adjusted for age and gender. A one-unit change in Lability/Negativity resulted in a participant being 19 times more likely to be a High bully.

The emotional regulation score of the ERC was tested in a similar model (see Model 5, Table 7). A test of the full model was found to be statistically significant $[X^2(3) = 18.53, p < .001]$. With all three variables included in the model, 72% of cases were correctly predicted; 80% of Low bullies; and 60% of High bullies were correctly predicted. Emotional regulation as reported by adults was a significant predictor of bullying group $[X^2(1) = 6.06, p = .01]$ when adjusted for age and gender. A one-unit change in emotional regulation resulted in a participant being 5.8 times *less* likely to be a High bully.

DISCUSSION

Bullying and Teasing

Teasing is not always bullying, but it can easily become so. Holding back on teasing is hard to do, especially where there is an appreciative audience

35

who may laugh at the child being teased. Sometimes when the target laughs along and takes the humor in stride, the edge goes out of the tease; but even when children know this in their heads, they are unlikely to practice it (Scambler et al., 1998). Adult mentors rated antisocial teasing and bullying as going hand in hand, such that a one-unit change in antisocial teasing resulted in a child being more than four times more likely to be a High bully. There is indeed a slippery slope of antisocial teasing into bullying. Contrary to our hypothesis, however, prosocial teasing was unrelated to bullying (i.e., correlation of $-.004$) and did not act as a protective factor against being a bully. Thus, if we saw a child at camp engage in fun, silly teasing with other children, we could not know one way or the other whether this child would engage in bullying when adults were not watching.

The CBS provided another way of measuring how children interacted with their peers. It was no surprise that scores on the Aggression with Peers subscale predicted bullying, as the behaviors described physical bullying: fights, kicks, bites, hits, etc. (Ladd & Proffitt, 1996). Scoring one point higher on the Aggression with Peers subscale raised a child's probability of being in the High bully group by 41 times. These behaviors are what people mean when they say someone is a bully. Importantly, though, bullying groups were also predicted—negatively—by positive aspects of children's behavior with their peers. Children who were high on the Prosocial with Peers subscale had a smaller change of being in the High bully group by about six times (per one unit change, Ladd & Proffitt, 1996). Here, we saw kind behaviors—helping, recognizing feelings, cooperating with peers—acting as protective factors against the potential meanness of bullying.

Emotion Regulation as a Mechanism Behind Bullying

A child's ability to regulate emotions was a strong predictor of whether a mentor viewed a child as a Low or High bully, suggesting a possible protective factor for children of incarcerated mothers who were successful in managing their emotions. Like Shields and Cicchetti (2001), the bullies had difficulties with emotion regulation. It was both the negative and the positive aspects of emotion regulation that told the story. The children whose moods flew up and down, showing more lability or negativity, had a higher chance of being classified as a High bully. Each point increase on the scale raised the odds almost 20 times. This held real and concrete meaning in our camp context. Children who are labile and negative are difficult to supervise and cause trouble with the other children waiting in line at the pool or getting to bed in a crowded cabin; it is likely that they are just as hard to live with at home and in the classroom. They show wide mood swings, frustration, and impulsivity, and they are prone to disruptive outbursts and tantrums (Shields & Cicchetti, 1997). The more positive subscale, which was appropriately named Emotion

Regulation, marked behaviors that included being a cheerful child who responds positively to overtures from peers and adults. These children laugh with their friends and quiet down when it is time for singing or announcements. This matched our previous findings with children at camp, in which positive and negative aspects of emotion regulation contributed in expected ways to externalizing behavior, internalizing behavior, and callous-unemotional traits (Lotze et al., 2010). These findings point to emotion regulation as a potential mechanism in the management of bullying and other problematic behavior in children who are already vulnerable because of family incarceration and life stressors.

Resilience and Children of Incarcerated Parents

Resilience is a dynamic process encompassing positive adaptation within the context of adversity (Luthar, Cicchetti, & Becker, 2000). Children of incarcerated parents certainly qualify as living with adversity. They most often experience living conditions that put them at risk (e.g., poverty, unstable home life), but parental incarceration adds strains to their well-being (Dallaire, 2007; Miller, 2006; Myers, Smarsh, Amlund-Hagen, & Kennon, 1999). Rutter (2006) has suggested that the research focus needs to be on individual differences and the causal processes they reflect, rather than on resilience as a general issue. Masten and Obradovic (2006) observed that recurring attributes of person, relationships, and context consistently emerge as predictors of individuals' resilience across diverse situations, and they name emotion regulation as a personal process that predicts resilience. Our findings lend support to this idea. Here, we have shown that poor emotion regulation is related to a child's hostile teasing and bullying, while positive emotion regulation is related to the capacity to refrain from these antisocial behaviors. Bullies are not resilient. Conversely, those children of incarcerated parents who maintain a calm and cheerful demeanor when playing with their peers, who restrict their teasing to kidding around, who laugh at others' gibes, and who refrain from bullying, are showing resilience.

Cause for Concern in Children of Incarcerated Parents

Our hope is that the children of incarcerated parents will be resilient and grow up strong, even when life is difficult. We know that resilience is characterized by an increased likelihood of positive outcomes in spite of risks to adaptation or development, and that resilience comes about through dynamic processes rather than static characteristics (Luthar et al., 2000). One of these processes involves accumulated risk (Garbarino, 1990). Garbarino suggested that vulnerability to risk increases as the number of stressful life events accumulate. He noted that when children are faced with four or five stressors, the likelihood of developing behavioral problems increases considerably. In prior studies with children of incarcerated mothers from the same summer camp, we counted the number of life stressors the children experienced in the past year (Hagen & Myers, 2003; Hagen et al., 2005; Mackintosh et al., 2006). Each year, at least half the children had experienced four or more risks, while some had up to 13 out of the 16 possible on the measure—and this did not count mothers' incarceration. Resilience is hard to achieve and maintain under the weight of such pressures.

The longer term outlook for children with incarcerated parents is troubling. Multiple studies find that as children of incarcerated parents become older, they are at heightened risk for antisocial behavior and arrest. Murray and Farrington (2005) examined adult children of parents who were incarcerated in the United Kingdom. These offspring were at increased odds for both juvenile conviction and adult incarceration. Parental incarceration had a stronger impact than other types of parent–child separation. Huebner and Gustafson (2007), using data from the National Longitudinal Survey of Youth, found that adult offspring of incarcerated mothers were more likely than peers to be involved in the criminal justice system. Finally, in a meta-analysis of 16 studies of parental incarceration, the authors concluded that children of incarcerated parents experienced about twice the risk for antisocial behavior and poor mental health as children of nonincarcerated parents (Murray et al., 2009). Although resilience breaks down for many of these children as they become adults, it is important to examine factors that may promote resilience.

In the present study, we examined emotion regulation as a possible protective factor. In her seminal work on resilience, Werner found that children who show resilience in the face of multiple risks have the ability to evoke positive attention from the people around them (Werner, 1993). Clearly those children who can manage their emotions effectively are more appealing. They are more likely to have real friends and develop close relationships with the surrogate caregivers who step in when the mother is imprisoned. On the other hand, the absence of emotion regulation skills is closely tied to problems in social competence (Calkins & Hill, 2007). Children who lack the ability to manage emotions effectively, whether they act out or withdraw, are harder to incorporate into a new home. When caregivers of children of incarcerated mothers see behavior as problematic, the caregivers also feel less warmth and acceptance for those children (Mackintosh et al., 2006).

Limitations

Our study was limited as a result of sampling and measurement issues. Only families who sent their children to camp were eligible to participate, and thus we know this was not a random sample of children of incarcerated mothers; we suspect that these children were in "better than average" situations, but do not have data from noncamping children to test that idea. We do not have data on mothers' incarceration history or her offenses, nor do we know whether fathers or other family members experienced incarceration. The sample was relatively small, limiting the power needed to conduct some analyses. Specifically, because of an insufficient sample size, we were not able to enter all the variables into a single analysis to test a full model. The measure of teasing was straightforward but not in-depth; we had no observational measures of children's teasing, nor were there measures from family members, teachers, or peers. Camp mentors rated the children on multiple measures, thus introducing a mono-informant and mono-method bias. And of course, as in any correlational study, it is not possible to assume causal direction.

Reflections

As researchers, our team gets to know these children in a summer camp setting, where they run, play, and sing, not unlike other children in our communities. We have an unusual relationship with our participants. Besides gathering data about them and from them, we eat, swim, and make bead necklaces with them. In our own experience, these children are more often cheerful than angry, more often kind than mean. But there are children every summer whose behavior is so aggressive, so out of bounds, that we are astounded. Some of the children are "almost impervious to camp rules and adult guidance" (Lotze et al., 2010, p. 713). Fighting, rock throwing, and vandalism happen before any adult can intervene. We work with children whose status as a bully is clear to both the adults and the other children (Shields & Cicchetti, 2001). As Olweus (1993) notes, unless it is modified early in life, bullying—and we would add, antisocial teasing—may be the beginning of a generally antisocial and rule-breaking behavior style that can extend into adulthood (i.e., Murray & Farrington, 2005; Murray et al., 2009). It is a favor to these children, and to our communities, to carefully monitor their teasing and prohibit their bullying.

Emotion regulation has potential importance as a mechanism for understanding resilience and long-term outcomes for children of incarcerated parents. Much of emotion regulation is shaped through socialization processes within the family: the emotional climate of the family, parent–child conversations (including discussions about the causes and consequences of feelings), the modeling of coping by the caregiver, and the overall quality of the caregiver–child relationship (Thompson & Meyer, 2007). Thus, effective interventions for emotion regulation optimally include the entire family. Supporting the emotion regulation of children affected by

39

parental incarceration is a worthy goal, though providing such support and impacting emotion regulation will not be easy to achieve given the difficult life histories and family situations of children whose parents are in prison or jail.

IV. ATTACHMENT REPRESENTATIONS OF IMPRISONED MOTHERS AS RELATED TO CHILD CONTACT AND THE CAREGIVING ALLIANCE: THE MODERATING EFFECT OF CHILDREN'S PLACEMENT WITH MATERNAL GRANDMOTHERS

Ann Booker Loper and Caitlin Novero Clarke

Maternal incarceration affects more than just the mother (Murray & Farrington, 2008; Poehlmann, Shlafer, Maes, & Hanneman, 2008). When a mother is incarcerated, particularly when she has functioned as the primary caregiver for her child, the structure of the family is disrupted. In most cases, child-rearing responsibilities are reorganized, with an individual other than the mother in charge of daily care, and mothers assume a secondary role (Baker, McHale, Strozier, & Cecil, 2010; Loper, Carlson, Levitt, & Scheffel, 2009). Although mothers may strive to maintain connection with their children, usually with the intention of postrelease reunification (Arditti & Few, 2008; Loper et al., 2009), contact with children undergoes dramatic change. A strong cocaregiving relationship may afford avenues for contact and communication that foster resilience in the family.

In the best of such circumstances, a cocaregiving relationship arises where both the mother and the new primary caregiver work together in alliance to raise the child (Cecil, McHale, Strozier, & Pietsch, 2008). This dyad has been likened to Minuchin's (1974) coparenting family structural framework between a husband and wife (Baker et al., 2010; Cecil et al., 2008) in which successful pairs cooperate, share power, and make mutually agreed-upon decisions (McHale, 2007; McHale et al., 2002). Under such circumstances, the child is thereby presented with a united coparenting support system with clear and consistent expectations (McHale, 2007). Whereas the coparenting structure for incarcerated mothers is distinct from that described by Minuchin, the same principles may apply to the

Corresponding author: Ann Booker Loper, University of Virginia, 417 Emmet Street South, Charlottesville, VA 22904, email: abl2x@virginia.edu

incarcerated mother's relationship with the child's caregiver (Baker et al., 2010; Cecil et al., 2008).

There are numerous challenges to developing a successful cocaregiving alliance when a mother is incarcerated (Baker et al., 2010). Correctional regulations substantially limit an incarcerated individual's communication with caregivers and children (Poehlmann et al., 2010). Phone usage is expensive and the duration and frequency of calls are limited. Often women are placed at facilities a far distance from their homes, contributing to difficulty regarding in-person visits. Caregivers themselves also may also pose a challenge to the development of the ideal cocaregiving alliance. In some cases, caregivers may take on absolute responsibility for the incarcerated parent's child, assuming the role as the gatekeeper between the mother and her child (Loper et al., 2009). The amount of communication the caregiver maintains is likely affected by the degree of trust or confidence that she has in the incarcerated mother, which itself may depend on maternal history of substance use and criminal activity (Hanlon, Carswell, & Rose, 2007; Smith, Krisman, Strozier, & Marley, 2004). Caregivers may also be unable, because of financial hardships or health problems, or otherwise unwilling to provide adequate care for the child, leading the incarcerated mother to assume infeasible responsibilities given the constraints of prison (Hayslip & Kaminski, 2005). Thus, the structure of the coparenting alliance ranges from situations where a mother has no involvement in her child's life and a caregiver has control of most of the parenting, to instances where the caregiver maintains a minimal role in raising the child and the mother is challenged to handle responsibilities from prison or jail (Baker et al., 2010). The ideal relationship would likely exist between these extremes and involve a unified collaboration between the incarcerated mother and her cocaregiving partner.

The mother also plays her own part in maintaining communication with her children (Arditti & Few, 2008; Loper et al., 2009). Many women report that preserving the relationship by regular and sustained contact with children is important to them, and that lack of communication leads to emotional distress and worry. However, several factors may contribute to a mother decreasing contact with her child through letter writing, phone calls, and requesting visits (Poehlmann et al., 2010). In particular, mothers describe visitation with their children as generating mixed emotions (Arditti & Few, 2008). Institutional rules often limit the amount of physical contact allowed between mother and child as well as the duration of the visit. Mothers are also sensitive to their children's distress at seeing them in the harsh setting of prison or jail, and often feel guilty and embarrassed (Arditti, 2003; Loper et al., 2009). While receiving a visit from the child has potential to be a positive experience for both mother and child, these factors may limit the extent to which mothers feel that they can connect with their children during visitation

(Arditti & Few, 2008). The emotional turmoil a mother experiences may be heightened when the visits are irregular or infrequent or if mothers feel that the child is not being properly supported throughout the visitation experience. The incarcerated mother's confidence in the caregiver's ability to provide frequent and regular visitation and to support the child during a potentially stressful visit might together impact the mother's requests for visitation. Similarly, if a mother feels that her child experiences phone calls and letters as a negative experience, or if she senses that the caregiver discourages communication, she may be reluctant to attempt contact by such means.

The relationships the mother maintains with her children and family throughout her incarceration can benefit her psychological well-being and ability to show resilience during the stress of incarceration (Houck & Loper, 2002; Loper et al., 2009; Poehlmann, 2005b; Tuerk & Loper, 2006). For example, a higher sense of alliance with her child's caregiver has been associated with lower depressive symptoms (Loper et al., 2009). Similarly, a reduction in parenting stress has been associated with more frequent mother–child communication through letters and phone calls (Houck & Loper, 2002). Children can be a great source of happiness and comfort for an incarcerated mother; hearing from children can bring joy and dispel some of the anguish and uncertainty she has about their well-being. Regular communication may also serve as a reminder of her role within the family. A sense of identity as a mother may play a role in rehabilitation efforts as mothers work toward release goals and ultimately reuniting with children (Arditti & Few, 2008). Daily or weekly communication may serve as a regular reminder of their reasons to keep working toward self-improvement by, for example, maintaining sobriety, taking vocational classes to gain job skills, or attending anger management classes.

The Role of the Incarcerated Mother's Own Early Maternal Relationship: An Attachment Perspective

When a mother is confronted with relinquishing responsibility of her child to another individual who assumes her previous role, her own recollected childhood experiences become salient and thus pertinent to her expectations for her own child. This supposition is based on the theory that repeated patterns of interactions between a young child and primary caregiver become internalized expectations, or an "internal working model," for others, as well as perception of self and others in future interactions (Bowlby, 1973; Main, Kaplan, & Cassidy, 1985). The development of a particular attachment pattern in childhood thereby depends on the consistency and quality of the caregiver's response to the child's needs, typically communicated through nonverbal means (Bowlby, 1973; Main et al.,

43

1985). In theory, an infant whose needs are met by a sensitive and responsive adult grows to form a secure attachment that leads to recall of warm and supportive interactions, and such mental representations are unconsciously activated in interactions with others. In contrast, an adult who recalls a harsh and punitive or inconsistent caregiver as a child is at risk for developing an insecure attachment and thus interacts with others guided by a similarly negative mental model.

The degree to which an individual has achieved a secure relationship, or recalls a warm and supportive relationship with a primary caregiver, can affect the ability to develop a successful coparenting relationship as outlined by Minuchin (1974). Maternal insecure attachment has been shown to predict higher levels of parental conflict (Talbot, Baker, & McHale, 2009). In contrast, individuals with secure attachments tend to exhibit effective problem solving behavior, are more collaborative, and are more proactive in regulating emotions during interpersonal conflict with partners (Bouthil-lier, Julien, Dube, Belanger, & Hamelin, 2002; Collins & Feeney, 2004; Crowell et al., 2002; Roisman et al., 2007). They are also less likely than adults with insecure attachments to perceive ambiguous actions of others as being negative, unsupportive, or hurtful (Collins & Feeney, 2004). Following emotionally stressful interactions, secure adults also tend to display less negative affect compared to insecure adults (Mikulincer & Florian, 1997).

Among samples of incarcerated mothers and fathers, studies have shown that more positive relationships between parents and caregivers are associated with higher levels of incarcerated parent–child contact. Poehlmann, Shlafer et al. (2008) found that when the cocaregiving relationship was more intimate, warm, and loyal, mothers and children spoke more often on the phone and mothers received more visits from their children. Along the same lines, Loper et al. (2009) found a positive association between a mother's sense of caregiver alliance and the amount of contact she had with her children.

Attachment relationships that are formed between infant and mother, who often functions as the primary caregiver, tend to have the greatest impact on adult attachment representations. However, few studies have examined the impact of a warm versus harsh recollection of a primary caregiver on the response of the individual to caregiving in situations that likely activate the attachment system (Simpson, Winterheld, Rholes, & Orina, 2007; Talbot et al., 2009). Incarceration is arguably a particularly strong activating trigger for the attachment system, as it involves a dramatic and sometimes lengthy separation from children, family, and community. If such disruption raises implicit memories of the incarcerated mother's own early attachment experiences, what happens if the source of those memories—her own mother—is now caring for her child?

Maternal Grandparent as Caregiver

To our knowledge, no study has directly contrasted the impact of child placement with the maternal grandmother versus placement with an alternate caregiver on child contact and coparenting alliance. In their survey of incarcerated parents, Glaze and Maruschak (2008) reported that, in contrast to the 45% of children of imprisoned mothers who were placed with a grandparent, nearly 11% of children of imprisoned mothers were in foster care and approximately 37% resided with the father. Given the possible problematic relationships that may occur between incarcerated mothers and their husbands (Arditti & Few, 2008), as well as the likely difficulties when children are placed in foster care, it is plausible that, in general, incarcerated mothers whose children are placed with the maternal grandparent might have stronger coparenting alliance and more contact than those in other placements.

However, the potential benefits posed by such child placement can be affected by the attachment patterns that have developed between the incarcerated mother and her own mother who assumes the caregiving role. The presumed activation of the attachment system when mothers are separated from children by incarceration may be intensified if the source of early attachment mental models is the child's caregiver. This context—placement of the child with the maternal grandmother—can evoke the incarcerated mother's feelings and thoughts regarding her child's experiences in a unique way. If the incarcerated mother recollects a warm and caring early relationship with her own mother, she may well maintain this view as the relationship shifts to a cocaregiving situation, and she anticipates that her child enjoys the same care and attachment that she herself experienced as a child. Such a situation could foster resilience processes in the child and family. In contrast, an incarcerated mother who recalls a contentious and cold childhood with her mother may maintain those perceptions following her incarceration. In conjunction with the theorized negative mental model of motherhood that results from the poor early attachment, the placement of the child with the source of this confused attachment history may result in intensified conflict in the coparenting alliance, thus contributing to the child's experience of risk during the mother's incarceration.

The Present Study

The purpose of this study was to investigate the relation between two potential correlates of an imprisoned mother's child–caregiver alliance and child contact: (1) an incarcerated mother's early attachment quality, as assessed by her recollected sense of warmth and acceptance by her own mother; and (2) the incarcerated mother's relationship to the caregiver (maternal grandmother vs. other caregiver). Consistent with previous research, we anticipated that placement of children with the maternal grandmother as well as perceived positive early attachment experiences would be associated with a more optimal coparenting alliance (Arditti & Few, 2008; Bouthillier et al., 2002; Collins & Feeney, 2004; Crowell et al., 2002; Roisman et al., 2007; Talbot et al., 2009). As a strong coparenting alliance is associated with higher levels of child contact for incarcerated samples (Loper et al., 2009; Poehlmann, Shlafer et al., 2008), we anticipated that effects would be present as well for contact measures. However, we focused our study on a potential interaction effect between these variables, such that the enhanced contact and alliance afforded by placement of children with the maternal grandmother would only be present if there was a collateral positive early attachment history between the incarcerated mother and her mother.

METHOD

Participants

Participants included 138 women incarcerated in a medium-security state prison. Women voluntarily attended an information session that described the current study as well as an additional study that evaluated a parenting educational program. Of approximately 1,100 women housed at the facility, 216 attended an initial general information session, and 154 returned to the follow-up meeting in which they filled out measures for the current study. Sixteen women were dropped from analyses due to incomplete data. The 16 women who had incomplete data included 8 women who did not indicate their relationship to their child's caregiver and 8 women who had incomplete information regarding at least one parenting measure. There were no noteworthy differences in terms of demographic or criminal characteristics between the remaining cohort of women with complete data and those who partially completed measures.

The sample included 51 women whose children were placed with their maternal grandmother, and 87 women whose children were placed with a caregiver other than the maternal grandmother. All measures were administered before implementation of a collateral study regarding parent education. As stipulated in the IRB approval of the study, we did not gather data concerning the nonconsenting women, and thus cannot describe the differences between the consenting and nonconsenting groups. Descriptive information regarding demographic information, criminal circumstances, as well as child-related information, is depicted in Table 8.

TABLE 8

Sample Description

	Frequency (%)
Race	
White	71 (51.8)
Black	56 (40.9)
Other	10 (7.3)
Education	
No high school	39 (29.3)
High school/GED	67 (50.4)
Some college	27 (20.3)
Marital status[a]	
Married	45 (33.3)
Separated	44 (32.6)
Always single	46 (34.1)
Offense	
Violent	46 (35.4)
Property	44 (33.8)
Drug	31 (23.8)
Other	9 (6.9)
Child gender[b]	
Male	62 (46.3)
Female	72 (53.7)
Lived with child before prison	105 (79.5)

	M (SD)
Inmate age (years)	32.8 (6.7)
Sentence length (months)	32.8 (6.8)
Child age (years)[b]	9.8 (4.6)
Number of minor children	2.2 (1.1)

[a]Married category includes common-law committed relationships.
[b]Refers to child referenced on the PAM (Parenting Alliance Measure).

Measures

Demographic and Child-Related Information

Imprisoned women completed a paper-and-pencil questionnaire regarding their age, race, marital status, and educational level. In addition, they indicated whether they had lived with their children prior to incarceration, the current age of children, and their number of children.

Caregiver Status

The caregiving relationship was coded as a dichotomous variable reflecting whether children resided with the imprisoned mother's own mother (maternal grandmother) versus placement with an alternate caregiver.

The mother version of the Adult Parental Acceptance Rejection Questionnaire (which we identify here as PARQ-M; Rohner, 2005) assessed the incarcerated mother's recollection of warmth, acceptance, and rejection from her own mother during her childhood. Participants responded to a series of 60 items about their own childhood such as "my mother made me feel what I did was important" and "my mother went out of her way to hurt my feelings." Participants responded to each item by selecting one of four responses ("almost always true"; "sometimes true"; "rarely true"; "almost never true"). Each response received a corresponding scores (1–4), while items reflecting perceptions of parental warmth and acceptance were reverse scored and all items summed so that lower total scores indicated more perceived warmth and acceptance from their own mother during their childhood. The measure yields a total score representing a parent's performance on the "Warmth Dimension of Parenting," (Rohner, Khaleque, & Cournoyer; 2005, p. 7). The Total Score, used in the present study, is the sum of four subscales (Warmth/Affection; Hostility/Aggression; Indifference/Neglect; Undifferentiated Rejection). To date, there has been no formal standardization of the instrument. However, Rohner (2005) reviewed numerous studies that have used the instrument, and reported that in the United States, PARQ-M total scores typically range between 90 and 110. The PARQ has been shown to be a reliable measure of adult perceptions of their childhood in both the general and incarcerated populations (Chyung, & Lee, 2008; Joo, 2008; Parmar & Rohner, 2005; Veneziano & Rohner, 1998). A meta-analysis of studies performed between 1977 and 2000 by Khaleque and Rohner (2002) reported internal consistencies of between .76 and .97 for Adult Total PARQ. For the present study Cronbach's alpha for the Total PARQ-M score was .98. To establish validity, Rohner (2005) compared subscales of the instrument to the content-relevant subscales of the Children's Report of Parenting Behavior Inventory (CRPBI; Schaefer, 1965) as well as the Bronfenbrenner Parental Behavior Questionnaire (BPB; Sielgelman, 1965) in a sample of 147 adult undergraduates. Rohner observed correlations ranging from .86 to .90 between the appropriately matched scales of the PARQ with the CRPBI, and a correlation of .43 between the Hostility subscale of the PARQ-M and the Physical Punishment subscale of the BPB.

Coparenting Alliance With Caregiver

The Parenting Alliance Measure (PAM; Abidin & Konold, 1999) captured the imprisoned mother's perceived coparenting alliance with her child's caregiver. The PAM is a 20-item self-report measure, originally developed to assess the working relationships between two parents. To make the measure more appropriate for the present study population, the wording was altered from "your child's other parent" to "your child's caretaker." As the measure is designed to reflect the coparenting relationship in relation to an individual child, mothers were directed to rate statements in regards to the caregiver of their minor child whose birthday came first during the calendar year. The measure uses a five-point Likert scale, ranging from "strongly disagree" to "strongly agree" for each of 20 items regarding concordance with the caregiver. The items are summed and higher scores indicate a more positive alliance between mother and caregiver. Abidin and Konold (1999) report a Cronbach's alpha of .97 for the PAM. Alpha for the measure in the present sample was .96. Abidin and Brunner (1995) demonstrated that the PAM has suitable convergent validity with other well-validated measures of parenting stress and relationship quality. In a combined sample of mothers and fathers, Abidin and Brunner found a correlation of $-.74$ between scores on the PAM and Total Parenting Stress scores as measured by the Stress Inventory for Parents of Adolescents (SIPA; Sheras, Abidin, & Konold, 1998). Similarly, the authors found the PAM to be correlated at .66 with the Cohesion scale of the Family Adaptability and Cohesion Evaluation III (FACES-III; Olson, Portner, & Lavee, 1985) and at .59 with the Dyadic Adjustment Scales (DAS; Spanier, 1976), which measures perceptions of relationship adjustment and satisfaction.

Contact With Children and Caregivers

Four individual items captured the degree of contact the imprisoned mother had with her child and child's caregiver. Mothers were queried regarding the frequency of letters they had written, phone calls to children, and consultation with the child's caregiver during the previous month on a five-point ordinal scale ("Every day"; "Every week"; "Every month"; "Few times a year"; "Never"). The same five-point ordinal scaling was used for an estimate of prison face-to-face visits with children during the previous year, but reflected whether there was contact "Once a month," "Between 6 to 11 times a year," "Between 2 and 5 times during the year," "Once," and "No such contact in the last year." Each item served as a separate dependent variable in the current study.

Analyses

Prior to conducting our primary analyses we conducted a series of correlation analyses in order to identify potential associations between demographic characteristics and each of the current major variables. As none were evident, we did not control for minority status, age, marital status, number of children, or educational level in any of the current analyses. As previously described, we dropped 16 women who had provided incomplete data, which enabled all analyses to be conducted with the same cohort of women.

Our primary analyses consisted of a series of regressions that evaluated the relation between caregiver status (Maternal Grandmother vs. Other Caregiver) and PARQ-M scores with each of the four separate contact variables (letter writing, phone calls, personal visits, consultation with caregivers) as well as with parenting alliance as measured by the PAM. For each regression, we focused attention on the interaction of caregiver status and PARQ-M scores to evaluate potential moderating effects associated with the women's relationship to the child caregiver. In order to more fully understand observed interaction effects, we followed the primary regression analyses with post-hoc comparisons of average scores for the previous dependent variables between four subgroups of the larger sample. These subgroups were divided according to mothers whose children were in either of the two caregiver groups, and then further subdivided by mothers who reported either high (upper third) or low (lower third) early warmth from their own mother.

RESULTS

A series of regressions evaluated the association between Caregiver Status and PARQ-M scores with each of the home contact variables as well as parenting alliance as measured by the PAM. The patterns were similar across each of the measures with the exception of letter writing. Placement of children with the maternal grandmother (vs. an alternate caregiver) was associated with more frequent phone contact, prison visitation, mother–caregiver child consultation, as well as a higher level of coparenting alliance, compared to placement with other caregivers. Likewise there was a positive relation between the imprisoned mother's recollected maternal warmth and acceptance during her childhood and these same dependent variables. However, for each of these variables, there was a significant interaction that indicated a conditional effect for the caregiver variable. The interaction effects were evaluated following Aiken and West's (1991) procedures for post-hoc probing of significant interactions. These procedures evaluate the separate simple slope lines for the two caregiver groups for the relation between PARQ-M scores and each of the dependent variables, and yield a t-value representing the comparison of each regression slope to zero. This probing indicated that the relation between early maternal warmth and current coparenting alliance and each of the child contract measures was observed only if children were placed with the maternal grandmother (PAM: $t = 4.77$, $p < .001$; Consultation with Caregiver: $t = 2.81$, $p < .01$; Phone Contact: $t = 2.86$, $p < .01$; Visitation Contact: $t = 3.82$, $p < .001$). By contrast, each of these relationships was nonsignificant for mothers whose children were placed with other caregivers. Results of the regression analyses and post-hoc probing are presented in Table 9.

TABLE 9

Summary of Regressions: Prediction of Contact and Coparenting Alliance by Caregiver
Status and Inmate Perceptions of Early Maternal Warmth

Dependent Variable	Multivariate F $(df = 3, 134)$	R^2	PARQ-M	Caregiver Status	Interaction PARQ-M by Caregiver	Conditional Effect of Child Caregiver MG	Other
Coparent alliance	$F = 10.32$	$.19^{***}$	$t = 4.63^{***}$	$t = 4.86^{***}$	$t = 4.17^{**}$	$t = 4.77^{**}$	ns
Contact—consult	$F = 5.39$	$.11^{**}$	$t = 2.78^{**}$	$t = 3.42^{**}$	$t = 2.56^{*}$	$t = 2.81^{*}$	ns
Contact—letters	ns		ns	ns	ns	ns	ns
Contact—phone	$F = 4.14$	$.08^{**}$	$t = 2.86^{**}$	$t = 3.17^{**}$	$t = 2.64^{*}$	$t = 2.86^{**}$	ns
Contact—visitation	$F = 5.31$	$.11^{**}$	$t = 3.78^{***}$	$t = 3.55^{**}$	$t = 3.47^{***}$	$t = 3.82^{***}$	ns

Note. PARQ-M = Adult Parental Acceptance and Rejection Questionnaire—Mother version; MG = maternal grandmother caregiver.
$^{*}p < .05.$ $^{**}p < .01.$ $^{***}p < .001.$

Letter writing was the exception to this pattern as it was unrelated to Caregiver Status. However, there was a trend effect, $t = 1.86$, $p = .06$, which suggested that letter writing to children was related to the mothers' sense of childhood warmth and acceptance from their own mothers.

In order to understand the pattern of performance more fully, we divided the sample into three groups based on their PARQ-M total scores. This trichotomy produced a group of 48 women who reported a Total Scale score less than 83 (High Early Warmth)[1] which we contrasted with a group of 50 women who reported scores of 120 or above (Low Early Warmth). Using Rohner's (2005) benchmark of scores between 90 and 120 as representing a typical range of performance on the measure, these two groups were therefore performing either above or below the usual scores for the measure. Each of these groups were then subdivided according to whether the child resided with the maternal caregiver versus another caregiver, resulting in four separate groups: Maternal Grandmother Caregiver + High Early Warmth (MGM-High); Maternal Grandmother Caregiver + Low Early Warmth (MGM-Low); Other Caregiver + High Early Warmth (Other-High); and Other Caregiver + Low Early Warmth (Other-Low). This subdivision of participants enabled a comparison of means between mothers who evidenced relatively low levels of maternal warmth and acceptance during their childhood from those with relatively higher levels of maternal warmth within each of the two child caregiver groups. As expected from the previous regression analyses, there was a significant univariate main effect for the comparison of the four groups on the PAM, $F(3, 94) = 5.71$, $p < .01$, $_{p}\eta^2 = .15$, and contact measures (Caregiver Consultation: $F(3, 94) = 4.85$, $p < .01$, $_{p}\eta^2 = .13$; Letters: $F(3, 94) = 1.58$, $p < .05$, $_{p}\eta^2 = .05$; Phone Calls: $F(3, 94) = 4.52$, $p < .01$, $_{p}\eta^2 = .13$; Personal visits: $F(3, 94) = 4.82$, $p < .01$,

51

TABLE 10

Dependent Variables for Whole Sample and High Early Warmth Versus Low Early Warmth Subsamples

		M (SD)			
		Maternal Grandmother Caregiver		Other Caregiver	
	All Participants ($N = 138$)	High Early Warmth ($n = 18$)	Low Early Warmth ($n = 16$)	High Early Warmth ($n = 30$)	Low Early Warmth ($n = 34$)
PAM	78.92 (18.62)	93.94 (6.31)	70.67 (19.27)	75.95 (19.58)	74.55 (24.56)
Contact-Consult	2.44 (1.26)	3.44 (0.98)	2.31 (1.30)	2.23 (1.00)	2.29 (1.34)
Contact-Letters	2.97 (1.01)	3.27 (1.07)	2.68 (0.87)	3.16 (0.91)	2.82 (1.11)
Contact-Phone	2.17 (1.90)	3.11 (1.13)	1.93 (1.12)	2.00 (1.02)	2.12 (1.23)
Contact-Visitation	2.99 (1.70)	4.44 (1.10)	2.43 (1.79)	3.20 (1.71)	3.09 (1.64)

Note. Low warmth, total PARQ-M (Adult Parental Acceptance Rejection Questionnaire—Mother version) score of 120 or higher; high warmth, total PARQ-M score of 82 or lower; PAM, parenting alliance measure. Higher scores on PAM (Parenting Alliance Measure) represent more positive coparenting alliance; Contact scores represent average for five-point scale single item rating; higher scores represent higher levels of contact; Contact-Consult, consultation with caregiver regarding child; Contact-Letters, frequency of inmate letters to child; Contact-Phone, frequency of phone calls to child; Contact-Visitation, frequency of personal in-prison visits.

$p\eta^2 = .13$). Post-hoc contrasts (see Tables 10 and 11) revealed a general pattern in which levels of contact and alliance for the imprisoned mothers who reported a close early attachment to their own mothers who now served as child caregivers significantly differed from the pattern for the imprisoned mothers in all three alternate groups. There were no evident differences

TABLE 11

Comparisons of Mothers Whose Children Are Placed With Maternal Grandmother and Who Recollect High Level of Early Warmth Versus Mothers in the Other Three Groups

	Alternate Groups as Compared to MGM-High		
	MGM-Low ($n = 16$)	Other-High ($n = 30$)	Other-Low ($n = 34$)
		t-Value	
PAM	4.61***	4.64***	4.86***
Contact-consult	2.83**	4.07***	3.21**
Contact-letters	1.76	0.38	1.43
Contact-phone	3.03**	3.51**	2.85**
Contact-visitation	3.89**	3.07**	3.55**

Note. All post-hoc t-tests of contrasts within the three alternate groups were nonsignificant. MGM-High, placement with maternal grandmother and perceived high level of early maternal warmth; MGM-Low, placement with maternal grandmother and perceived low level of early maternal warmth; Other-High, placement with other caregiver and perceived high level of early maternal warmth; Other-Low, placement with other caregiver and perceived low level of early maternal warmth.
**$p < .01$. ***$p < .001$.

between imprisoned mothers in the three alternate groups (placement with maternal grandmother and low recollected maternal warmth; placement with other caregiver and high recollected maternal warmth; placement with other caregiver and low recollected maternal warmth).

The PAM provides normative information regarding parenting alliance scores (Abidin & Konold, 1999). Based on this, the average PAM score for mothers whose children resided with maternal grandmother and who reported high early maternal warmth was at the 85th percentile. By contrast, mothers in the three remaining groups evidenced lower parenting alliance (MGM-Low = 32nd percentile; Other-High = 39th percentile; Other-Low = 38th percentile).

DISCUSSION

The present study found that an imprisoned mother's sense of warmth and acceptance by her own mother was associated with a more positive coparenting alliance with her child's caregiver. This effect is consistent with previous research as well as with the theoretical notion that early positive attachment experiences can pave the way toward more positive interpersonal relationships in adulthood (Crowell et al., 2002; Collins & Feeney, 2004; Talbot et al., 2009), thus contributing to resilience processes in high-risk families. However, the apparent benefit was not uniform throughout the sample. Effects were moderated by children's placement, with the positive association evident only if children were placed with the maternal grandmother. A similar pattern occurred in terms of contact with children. There was a positive relation between child contact and the mother's sense of childhood maternal connection and warmth, but the effect was conditional on whether children were placed with their maternal grandmother. This general pattern is consistent with the notion that when an imprisoned mother perceives a more secure early relationship with her mother, she feels assured that her child is being well cared for and thus expresses confidence and support of the home caregiver. This alliance is further strengthened by steady child contact experiences afforded by the home caregiver. Because many children of imprisoned mothers live with their maternal grandmothers (e.g., Glaze & Maruschak, 2008), these findings are important in furthering our understanding of potential protective factors in a subgroup of children with incarcerated parents.

Our post-hoc analyses grouped imprisoned mothers into categories of high versus low early maternal warmth and acceptance, which were cross-referenced with caregiver placement status. Inspection of the means for each of the four resulting groups revealed that the patterns for imprisoned mothers who recollected early warmth and whose child was placed with their own mother were distinct from the three remaining groups, who were similar in terms of contact and alliance. Specifically, mothers who reported higher early maternal warmth but whose children were placed with someone other than their own mother were not distinct from those who reported low maternal acceptance and warmth, regardless of caregiver status. Thus, for mothers with children placed with other caregivers, the theorized benefits of having a more positive childhood did not distinguish them in terms of alliance and child contact from those who experienced a harsher childhood. The apparent more positive connection and alliance occurred only if both conditions—early maternal warmth and acceptance and maternal grand-mother placement—were present.

Inspection of the standardization information from the PAM (Abidin & Konold, 1999) indicates a relatively high level of reported coparenting alliance (the 85th percentile of the standardization group) for imprisoned mothers who reported childhood warmth and acceptance by their own mother who now cared for their children. By contrast, the alliance scores of the three remaining groups were consistent with a low-average level of coparenting alliance (from the 32nd to 39th percentile of the standardization group). As the measure does not afford separate norms for clinical or prison samples, it is not possible to evaluate how such scores line up in terms of the larger prison population. Nonetheless, the difference between the groups is clinically important and further supports the notion that the distress that is associated with this challenging coparenting arrangement may be lessened if the imprisoned mother is able to trust, based on her own experiences, that her child is well cared for.

The sole exception to the current pattern of effects was for letter writing. Previous studies have emphasized the value of letter writing as a mode of communication with children that is safe, inexpensive, and less subject to the emotional volatility that is possible during phone or personal visits (Loper et al., 2009; Tuerk & Loper, 2006). In the present study, caregiver status was not related to the imprisoned mother's frequency of sending mail home to children. However, letter writing is a unique form of communication with children, as it does not depend upon the cooperation of the caregiver and is fully within the control of the incarcerated individual. There was a trend ($p = .06$) for mothers who sensed early warmth and acceptance to more frequently write letters to children. While not statistically significant, this trend is consistent with an attachment perspective regarding the importance of early maternal warmth and acceptance in forging a beneficial mental model of motherhood. It is plausible that mothers who experienced feelings of maternal warmth as a child developed a more nurturing model of parenting that provided the confidence and ability to maintain child communication by using this forum of contact that is less affected by the caregiver's cooperation. However, this speculation needs confirmation in future studies.

Separation from children because of incarceration is one of the most significant of the stresses of being in prison for incarcerated mothers, who frequently report sadness and concerns for the welfare of their children (Arditti & Few, 2008). Moreover, imprisonment, by definition, represents a form of abandonment of the incarcerated woman as she is forcibly separated from community and loved ones. It is reasonable to expect that this context could conjure an incarcerated mother's own recollected experiences of attachment or abandonment as a child. The present results imply that recollections of early maternal warmth and caring are particularly salient if the source of the early attachment patterns—the woman's own mother—is the child's caregiver. Specifically, the predicted relation between early maternal attachment, as approximated by recollected feelings of maternal warmth and acceptance, and coparenting connection and alliance occurred only when children were placed with the maternal grandparent. Results imply that for the imprisoned mothers who recalled a childhood that lacked warmth and acceptance by the individual who now cares for her child, there is a sense of disconnection that interferes with a successful coparenting alliance. By contrast, incarcerated mothers who feel secure in their own attachment to the individuals caring for their children are reassured for their children's welfare and are able to form positive coparenting relationships. Additional research should be conducted examining whether children in such households are protected from some of the negative effects of maternal imprisonment.

The general negative effects of parental incarceration on children and families are well known (Murray & Farrington, 2008), and recent studies have explored the potential impact that the cocaregiving relationship has on children raised by nonparental caregivers following parental incarceration (Baker et al., 2010; Poehlmann, 2003, 2005a). For example, in a study of 40 mothers in jail, Baker et al. found that communication between mothers and caregiving grandmothers involving more cooperation (empathy, validation, listening, and agreement) and less conflict (dismissal, disparagement, defensiveness, competition, and hostility) was associated with less attention and behavior problems among children. These findings are similar to those demonstrated in studies of working relationships between mothers and grandmothers in the general population (Brody, Flor, & Neubaum, 1998). In general population studies, it has been well-documented that better functioning relationships between adults contributes positively to emotional control, communication, and prosocial behavior of the children in their care, whereas children cared for by adults with discordant alliances are at increased risk for aggression, anxiety, withdrawal, and poor social competence (see McHale, 2007, for a review). Further, there is a greater likelihood of secure parent–child attachments among children who are presented with a united cocaregiving front (Caldera & Lindsey, 2006; Finger, Hans, Berstein, & Cox, 2009; Frosch, Mangelsdorf, & McHale, 2000; Owen & Cox, 1997). Thus, fostering positive coparenting alliances between incarcerated parents and caregivers could be explored as one means of fostering resilience in children with incarcerated parents.

There are several limitations that need to be considered in this study. The correlational patterns do not reveal causal direction of effects. It is plausible that the imprisoned mothers' recollected warmth and affection of the caregiving grandmother were constructed based on present experience of having greater opportunities for contact with children. Grandmothers who are able to provide multiple opportunities for contact may be perceived in a more positive light by imprisoned mothers, who then project a rosier picture of their own early life with this person. Along similar lines, because corroborative reports from the caregiver regarding alliance and contact were unavailable, the present study relies on self-report regarding the coparenting relationship from the sole perspective of the mother. Our measure of perceived early warmth, though well-validated and reliable, is not equivalent to more extensive clinical interviews, such as the Adult Attachment Interview (AAI), which carefully probes an adult regarding recollected childhood experiences with significant attachment figures (Main & Goldwyn, 1998). Future research of attachment patterns among incarcerated mothers with more individualized measures such as the AAI, as well as information from the collaborating caregiver would be valuable in understanding this most frequent context of child placement for children of incarcerated mothers.

As placement of children with the maternal grandmother is the most typical pattern for incarcerated mothers (Glaze & Maruschak, 2008), it is important to consider how to best build positive coparenting relationships among this substantial subgroup. The present results suggest possible benefits of this caregiving arrangement when the imprisoned mother perceives that her children are in the hands of a caregiver whom she knows, firsthand, to be capable of providing warmth and support. As a group, incarcerated women experience considerable childhood distress and trauma. An essential aspect of recovery for many incarcerated women is dealing with the consequences of disrupted early attachment patterns (Loper & Levitt, 2010). However, the present results suggest that this healing may be particularly important for imprisoned mothers who perceive that the same individuals who rejected them as children now care for their own children. Intensified efforts to understand the role of the early relationship between the caregiving grandmother and her incarcerated daughter may provide important benefits in forging a better context for collaborative efforts toward the child's welfare.

NOTE

1. For the PARQ-M, low scores reflect higher levels of warmth and acceptance.

56

V. TRIADIC INTERACTIONS IN MOTHER–GRANDMOTHER COPARENTING SYSTEMS FOLLOWING MATERNAL RELEASE FROM JAIL

James P. McHale, Selin Salman, Anne Strozier, and Dawn K. Cecil

Within every child's family, the nature of the relationship that evolves between the adults who assume responsibility for the child's care and upbringing—the family's coparenting alliance—will come to play a critically important role in that child's behavioral, social, and emotional adjustment (McHale & Lindahl, 2011). Coparenting alliances characterized by communication, cooperation, and coordination can be an unparalleled resource for the young child, providing consistent and predictable support for coping and adaptive efforts. By contrast, alliances marked by disconnection or dissonance can actually exacerbate child problems as nonsupport and unpredictability trigger anxiety, noncompliance, and other signs of adjustment problems. Strong and functional coparenting alliances are especially critical for children separated from a parent. During separations, the nature of the alliance between the absent mother and the child's other caregivers can affect the extent to which the child copes successfully or becomes distressed and disorganized. Child advocates and helping professionals are in need of approaches that can help them evaluate and understand the dynamics of coparenting alliances in families of young children affected by maternal incarceration. This report presents a promising method for assessing coparenting behavior in multigenerational families where mothers have recently been released from jail.

National data indicate that when mothers are incarcerated, children not fostered outside of the family are far more likely to be placed in the care of maternal grandmothers than they are to be cared for by fathers (Johnson & Waldfogel, 2004). Only 28% of incarcerated mothers report that their children are cared for by their fathers (Mumola, 2000), in large part because

---

Corresponding author: James P. McHale, Family Study Center, USF St. Petersburg, St. Petersburg, FL 33701, email: jmchale@mail.usf.edu

the preponderance of children with incarcerated mothers—75%, by some estimates (Phillips, Erkanli, Keeler, Costello, & Angold, 2006)—also have criminally involved fathers. While fathers do remain involved in many children's lives, at least from a distance, it is more uncommon that they play a sustained role as an ongoing, active caregiving figure.

Little is presently known about the dynamics of the coparenting alliances that evolve between incarcerated mothers and grandmothers. However, studies of coparenting in other family systems point to the unique role that observation can play in detecting several core coparenting dynamics in families, including cooperation, conflict, and disconnection. Triangular interactions between two coparents and a child, in particular, evoke well-worn family "scripts" that afford insights into propensities of the adults to support and enable one another's work with the child, to oppose one another's efforts, or in some cases to abdicate responsibility (Fivaz-Depeursinge & Corboz-Warnery, 1999; McHale, 1995; McHale & Fivaz-Depeursinge, 1999; Minuchin, 1974). Coparenting support and solidarity during triadic interactions has been linked to child adjustment in both contemporaneous and longitudinal studies of families with infants, toddlers, preschoolers, and elementary-aged children, while coparenting dissonance during triadic interactions has been prospectively linked to both internalizing and externalizing behavior problems in young children (see McHale & Lindahl, 2011, for a comprehensive review of this amassing literature). To date, however, no observational study of the coparenting dynamics exhibited between criminally involved mothers, coparenting grandmothers, and children during triadic family interactions has been conducted.

Developing a fuller understanding of how mothers and grandmothers work together—or do not—as coparents stands as a critically important advance for a research agenda concerned with understanding resilience processes in children of incarcerated parents and their families. Triadic observations hold promise for revealing which families possess the capacity to play a protective, buffering role for children, which families struggle to show such teamwork, and which actually do damage to children by virtue of a chaotic or hostile-competitive coparenting dynamic. In this report, we detail an observational investigation of triangular interactions involving recently released mothers, caregiving grandmothers, and preschool and kindergarten-aged children. The process of adapting a widely used triadic evaluation system (the Coparenting and Family Rating System) for this population is described, and preliminary data on reliability and validity are presented. Summaries of the dynamics of the study's 13 families are then provided. We close by commenting on the degree to which overall findings are similar or different from other populations, and describe implications for further research and for intervention strategies.

METHOD

Participants

Thirteen families, all with a child between the ages of 3 and 6 years, took part in the study. All children had a mother who had been incarcerated in a county jail between 3 and 6 months, with a release 1–2 months prior to the family assessment. The 13 women had been sentenced for a variety of charges ranging from driving with a suspended license to aggravated assault with a deadly weapon. Since most were detained on multiple charges, the most serious charge was used to establish types of offenses that brought the 13 women to jail. Five served time for violent offenses; 5 for drug offenses; 1 for property crime; and 2 for public order offenses. Total number of incarcerations, including the index incarceration for this study, ranged from 1 to 6. All 13 children studied had been cared for by their maternal grandmothers during the mother's incarceration. In 7 families, mothers and grandmothers were European American. In 5 of the 7 families (3 girls, 2 boys), the child was also European American; in the other 2 (both girls), the child was of mixed race, with an African American father. In the remaining six families, mothers, grandmothers, and children (3 boys and 3 girls) were African American. All 13 families lived below the federal poverty line.

Mothers ranged in age from 19 to 28. Most had moved in and out of children's lives during their early years, and 12 of the 13 mothers reported two or more different living situations during the child's lifetime (range 1–9). Importantly, however, all 13 mothers had spent at least 12 of the first 18 months of their child's life together with the baby, indicating the likelihood that mother–infant attachments had been formed. Grandmothers ranged in age from 41 to 68. All 13 had been involved in the children's lives as coparents prior to the index incarceration, and in all but two cases, their involvement had kept the children out of foster care. In the two families where children had had a foster placement, time in the system had been brief and the child had been quickly placed in the grandmother's care. Only one mother had had parental rights formally terminated, although she was living with the child and grandmother at the time of assessment. Though the study targeted families in which maternal grandmothers served as primary coparents, there was no intentional effort to exclude families if fathers were also involved. However, among the 13 families constituting this sample, fathers were not regularly accessible or participatory cocaregivers in any family.

Design and Procedure

Mothers and grandmothers were engaged in the study during the mother's incarceration, and all agreed to a videotaped home visit with the child following the mother's release. In the family home, researchers worked with the family to identify an area relatively free from distractions where a triadic play interaction could be videotaped. Though efforts were made to minimize noise and intrusions by other family members, neighbors, and pets, these efforts met with only partial success, and so data must be interpreted in light of the realities of the family's day-to-day residential realities. In all 13 families, however, there was successful completion of the full battery of tasks.

Home visits had two parts: (a) a family interaction involving mother grandmother and child; and (b) individual assessments, during which mothers and grandmothers completed individual interviews and reported on the child's behavioral adjustment, while the child completed an assessment in a separate area of the residence. The family interaction tasks were based on procedures used in earlier studies by the first author and other family researchers (e.g., Cowan & Cowan, 1992). They included a story-telling task; a family art project, in which the three family members created a mural of the family; a challenging puzzle task similar to the Weschler Intelligence Scale for Children (WISC) Block Design; and a delay-of-gratification task, in which an attractively wrapped gift was placed outside of the child's reach as the child waited with mother and grandmother for 5 min. A camera was set up so as to capture the threesome as they interacted with each other; the researchers left the room during tasks so family members could work in relative privacy. On average, the family interaction took 20 min (5 min per task). Following the task, the adults individually completed one-on-one assessments, while an examiner administered the Berkeley Puppet Interview to the child.

Measures

Coparenting During the Triadic Interaction

Videotaped records of the family interactions were evaluated by two researchers expert using the Coparenting and Family Rating System (CFRS; McHale, Kuersten-Hogan, & Lauretti, 2000), a global coding system widely used in evaluating coparenting dynamics of two-parent families during triadic interactions. The CFRS has been validated in numerous studies involving families with children of the age of those in this report (McConnell & Kerig, 2002; McHale et al., 2000). Core CFRS codes (cooperation, competition, verbal sparring, warmth, investment, and child-centeredness), described extensively elsewhere (McHale et al., 2000), capture elements of supportive, antagonistic, and disconnected interparental behavior during engagement with the child, and can be coded reliably.

Because the CFRS has never been previously used in work with family systems with an incarcerated parent, a two-step process was used to adapt the system for use with the current population. First, the CFRS manual's developer (the first author) and a coder expert in use of the system (the second author) used the CFRS manual and codes to informally evaluate three randomly chosen mother–grandmother–child triadic interactions. The standard CFRS rating process of taking notes about critical events relevant to each of the CFRS' core variables was followed, notes taken independently were compared, and aspects of the interactions not captured well by existing CFRS codes were identified and discussed. This discussion led to the drafting of two new global codes (Disengagement and Shared Focus), and a third new code (Coparenting Alliance) conceptualized as an overall summary rating specific to this population. These codes will be described below. With the final system in place, the two original coders independently and formally rated all 13 families. As is standard in use of the CFRS, all discrepancies in ratings were conferenced before arrival at a final consensus score for each family. These scores were then used as a gold standard, and inter-rater reliability was established with a third, blind coder. Reliabilities (intraclass correlations) fell within acceptable bounds for all variables, ranging from .72 (Shared Focus) to .88 (Verbal Sparring).

Brief thumbnail descriptions of the core CFRS codes and the three newly added codes, along with descriptive data for families in the sample, follow.

Cooperation (M = 3.62, SD = 1.33, range = 1–5). In cooperative families, partners accommodate and support one another's interactions with the child. Low-end ratings reflect the absence of any active support or cooperation between parents. High-end ratings reflect multiple instances of active collaboration, validation and support throughout the triadic interaction.

Competition (M = 1.77, SD = 1.36, range = 1–5). Competitive families are those that cannot refrain from intruding upon one another's interactions with the child. Low-end ratings signify families that refrain from any antagonistic or competitive behavior during all parts of the interaction; high-end ratings are given to families exhibiting repeated competitive behavior.

Verbal Sparring (M = 2.00, SD = 1.15, range = 1–5). Verbal sparring is a measure of overt disagreement and/or criticism expressed by the adults toward one another (not the child). High-end scores describe adults who express multiple criticisms throughout the interaction; low-end scores describe adults able to refrain from doing so.

Warmth (Mother–child M = 4, SD = 1.78, range = 1–7; Grandmother–child M = 4.15, SD = 1.34, range = 1–6; Mother–grandmother M = 3, SD = 1.47, range = 1–5). On the CFRS warmth is coded separately for each dyad in the family (mother–child; grandmother–child; mother–grandmother). High warmth connotes high levels of positive affect, animation, and enjoyment of one another. Inter-adult warmth is typically evinced through humorous comments, episodic mutual smiles and eye contact, simultaneous spontaneous laughter, and the like. Low-end scores are assigned if adults are unusually reserved and out of synch with the child and/or if they are disconnected as partners to one another (interacting only through the child, and without demonstrating any genuine humor or shared warmth). High-end warmth scores are given judiciously and only when there are clear and multiple moments of positive affective connection.

Investment (Mother M = 4.15, SD = 1.63, range = 1–7; Grandmother M = 4.38, SD = 1.04, range = 2–6). The CFRS includes a code for investment, or level of engagement with the child, by each of the two adults. High-end scores signify over-involvement and intrusiveness; mid-range scores signify a more optimal balance between engagement and monitoring; and low-end scores signify under-involvement with the child. These dyadic (parent–child) scores can then be used to calculate an Investment Discrepancy score ($M = 1.15$, $SD = 1.41$, range $= 0$–4). Discrepancy Scores of 0 signify coparents involved at similar levels; higher scores signify a tendency toward over-involvement by one adult, under-involvement by one adult, or both of these circumstances. In published work using the CFRS, its authors caution that the Investment Discrepancy score is not an index of clinically significant disengagement or enmeshment.

Child-Centeredness (M = 2.46, SD = 1.05, range = 1–4). A child-centered family is one in which the flow of the interaction follows the leads, interests, and initiatives of the child. A low child-centered (or, parent-centered) family is one in which the adults unilaterally direct the flow and tempo of the session. Mid-range scores signify either a balanced interaction (adults often leading but also attending to the child), or one in which no clearly apparent initiator of the session's flow (parent or child) can be determined.

Disconnection ($M = 2.08$, $SD = 1.38$, range $= 1$–5) assessed degree of family member detachment from emotional/attentional involvement for one or more extended periods (i.e., longer than 5 sec). This newly added code was necessary to properly characterize the emotional climate observed in certain families observed and discussed during the first stage of the work. As described above, the standard CFRS investment discrepancy score was not designed to be an index of clinically significant disengagement. The new Disconnection measure provides a direct index of problematic levels of disconnection and nonparticipation.

Shared Focus ($M = 3$, $SD = 1.68$, range $= 1$–5) was designed to assess how much the mother, grandmother and child were able to coordinate and sustain their *attention* as a single unit co-acting together, on a scale from 1 (never) to 5 (frequently). Families showing a strong Shared Focus did not simply work on the same task at the same time in parallel—most did this. Rather, family members showed synchronized and *joint* attention on a *single* object or action of focus. High scores on this scale required that coparents not only effectively solicit and scaffold the child's interest and attention on a common task, but also stay in synch with one another so that a sustained threesome focus could occur (Fivaz-Depeursinge & Corboz-Warnery, 1999). The CFRS Child-Centeredness variable failed to capture this important aspect of coparental work—remaining sensitive to the child (child-centeredness) *but also* planning and working together to provide the necessary degree of scaffolding (adult-centeredness).

Coparenting Alliance was designed as a population-specific scale to capture the overall status of the observed alliance between mother and grandmother. Drawing on Minuchin's (1974) concept of the coparental alliance as the family's "executive subsystem," the Coparenting Alliance scale's emphasis was on mutual cooperation and leadership seen between the two women. Coparenting Alliance was rated on a one to five continuum scale ranging from very problematic (Harmful) to very effective (Mutually Supportive). Hierarchy was one consideration in making determinations about the overall Alliance; families receiving highest scores (Mutually Supportive) shared coordination, had mutually cooperative influence, sensitively responded to child needs, and provided appropriate task scaffolding. In families where one person displayed more authority than the other, the highest score possible was not given because the two did not mutually co-lead and guide the interaction. However, a high-end score of 4 (Led/Supportive) was still assigned so long as the alliance impressed as a functional one the "second in command" behaved in a supportive, engaged manner.

In other families, a "led" adaptation signaled an altogether different dynamic. Such was the case when a coparent with less authority disconnected from the interaction or displayed behavior detrimental to or undermining of the joint interaction. In Strained alliances (scores of 3), Weak alliances (2), and Harmful/Damaging alliances (1), there were significant problems of the threesome in working together as a unit. In Strained Alliances, some hopeful elements indicative of family cohesion intermingled with disarray and problematic elements in structuring or accurately reading child signals. In families receiving even lower scores, shared focus was virtually absent altogether, either because of substantial disconnection by one or more family members (2) and/or because the unit showed no evidence of effective leadership (1). Leadership problems included high levels of competition and wrestling for control, or lack of any effective structuring and authority exerted by either woman.

Coparenting Cooperation and Conflict Revealed Through Interviews

During the individual portion of the assessment session, each woman was interviewed about how well she and her family member worked together as a coparenting team. Both the coparenting interview and the evaluation process are described in detail in Strozier, Armstrong, Skuza, Cecil, and McHale (2011). After qualitative coding, five-point rating scales were used to evaluate (a) overall degree of coparenting cooperation described by the interviewees; and (b) overall degree of coparenting conflict. Cooperation ($M = 3.33$, $SD = 1.14$, range $= 1$–5) was in evidence when interviewees conveyed respect for the other person's rights to parent, knew and *expressed something convincingly positive* about the other's parenting, and portrayed the coparenting relationship as one in which the two women did sometimes *talk together* about the child and at *least occasionally work collaboratively* to try to provide a unified front to the child. Scores could range from 1 (no evidence for any coparenting cooperation whatsoever) to 5 (convincing evidence that both interviewees not only knew and respected the other's parenting beliefs and skills, but also maintained a commitment to pulling together to try to help the child as a team). Conflict ($M = 3.42$, $SD = 1.06$, range $= 1–5$) captured the degree of discontent, criticism, and pessimism in the interviews of women when asked about the coparenting relationship and teamwork between the two women. Scores ranged from 1 (no evidence of conflict in either interview) to 5 (multiple instances of criticism and unresolved conflict expressed by both women).

Child SelfConcept

Children's self-perceptions in the realms of social competence, peer acceptance, depression–anxiety, and aggression–hostility were assessed by the Berkeley Puppet Interview (BPI; Ablow & Measelle, 1993). The BPI is an age-appropriate method using puppets to query children about key aspects of their lives. The interview was administered by a trained examiner in accordance with a standardized set of instructions. Two of the six BPI scales (academic competence and achievement motivation) were not administered given the young age of some participating children. Scores on the remaining four scales (social competence, peer acceptance, depression–anxiety, and aggression–hostility) were combined and averaged to form an overall selfconcept score. Support for the method's validity has been provided by Measelle, Ablow, Cowan, and Cowan (1998), who describe convergence between children's selfperceptions and ratings by adult informants as well as standardized test scores.

Child Behavior Problems

Mothers and grandmothers rated child behavior problems on the Child Behavior Checklist (CBCL), and CBCL Internalizing and Externalizing Problems broadband scale scores were calculated. The CBCL contains a list of behaviors rated on a three-point scale from 0 (*not true*) to 2 (*very true or often true*). Its Internalizing scale measures problematic behavior related to shyness, withdrawal, anxiety, and depression. Its Externalizing scale measures problematic behaviors related to attention, hyperactivity, defiance, and aggression. In several samples similar to this one, these scales have shown adequate reliability and validity (Achenbach & Ruffle, 2000). Eleven of 13 children were rated in the clinical range (T of 60 or greater) by their mother, grandmother, or both on at least one of the two behavior problem scales. However, the two women showed poor agreement in rating child internalizing behavior ($r = -.14$, ns) and only moderately better agreement in rating externalizing behavior ($r = .44$, ns).

RESULTS

Validity of the CFRS Coding

With a sample of 13 families, quantitative analyses were completed principally to examine directions of effects and establish whether CFRS codes behaved in a manner similar to those charted in other studies. Two sets of analyses are of interest. In the first, we examined validity of the new CFRS Coparenting Alliance summary code by comparing the *interview-based* Coparenting Cooperation and Conflict scores for the six families receiving scores of 4 (Led/Supportive) or 5 (Mutually Supportive) on the CFRS measure with those scored as 1 (Damaging), 2 (Weak) or 3 (Strained). These analyses indicated that the six families with higher CFRS Coparenting Alliance scores received significantly higher interview-based ratings on Coparenting Cooperation ($M = 3.86$, compared to $M = 3.00$ for families receiving lower scores, $F(1, 11) = 5.89$, $p < .05$, $\eta^2 = .40$). They also revealed less Coparenting Conflict during interviews ($M = 2.75$, compared to $M = 3.43$, $F(1, 11) = 2.36$, ns, $\eta^2 = .21$)—also in the hypothesized direction but short of statistical significance.

We also examined associations between CFRS variables and BPI and CBCL scores. Two variables—CFRS Cooperation ratings ($r = .64$, $p < .05$) and Investment Discrepancy scores ($r = -.69$, $p < .05$) were significantly correlated with children's selfconcept scores. That is, greater observed cooperation and less imbalance in the women's engagement with the child during the triadic play session were both associated with greater child selfconcept. Correlations between BPI scores and the remaining CFRS variables— Coparenting Alliance ($r = .37$), Competition ($r = -.11$), Verbal Sparring ($r = -.27$), Disengagement ($r = -.35$), and Shared Focus ($r = .39$) were also all in the hypothesized directions, though not statistically significant.

Grandmaternal CBCL ratings and maternal CBCL Externalizing scores were not associated with any of the CFRS ratings. Maternal ratings of higher Internalizing symptomatology were significantly associated with more Disengagement ($r = .61$, $p < .05$) and less Shared Focus ($r = -.59$, $p < .05$) during the triadic interaction. Two other CFRS variables (Coparenting Alliance; $r = -.33$) and Cooperation ($r = -.34$) were also associated with Internalizing ratings in the hypothesized direction, but not statistically significant. Perhaps of greater interest, despite the very poor overall agreement between mothers and grandmothers in rating children's Internalizing symptoms, the degree of discrepancy between maternal and grandmaternal CBCL Internalizing ratings was significantly *less* ($M = 7.0$) among families rated as 4 or 5 on the new CFRS Coparental Alliance index than among families rated as 1, 2, or 3 ($M = 14.4$; $F(1, 11) = 5.79$, $p < .05$. That is, among Led/ Supportive and Mutually Supportive Coparental Alliances, the two women *saw the child similarly*. Hence despite the small N, several indicators suggest that CFRS scales captured meaningful variability in coparenting behavior.

Qualitative Analyses: Coparenting Dynamics

In this final section, we provide brief narrative descriptions of the coparenting dynamics of each of the 13 families, using the new Coparenting Alliance score as an organizing rubric. CFRS scores central to determinations made for each family are outlined in Table 12, with key observations reflected in and integrated into qualitative descriptions provided for each family.

TABLE 12

RATINGS OF TRIADIC INTERACTIONS ACCOMPANIED BY MOTHER/GRANDMOTHER CHILD BEHAVIOR CHECKLIST

	1	2	3	4	5	6	7	8	9	10	11	12	13
Age													
Child	5	4	5	3	3	3	4	4	3	6	6	3	3
Mother	26	33	—	21	25	19	24	28	23	26	25	21	22
CFRS domains													
Coparenting alliance	5	5	5	5	5	4	3	3	2	2	2	1	1
Cooperation	5	4	4	5	5	5	4	4	1	2	3	2	3
Competition	1	2	1	1	1	3	4	1	1	1	1	5	1
Verbal sparring	2	1	1	1	2	2	3	2	1	2	3	5	1
Mother investment	5	5	4	4	5	5	7	4	1	1	4	5	4
Grandmother investment	5	5	5	4	5	5	4	4	5	4	3	6	2
Investment discrepancy	0	0	1	0	0	0	3	0	4	3	1	1	2
Warmth btw M-C	5	4	3	5	6	5	7	3	1	1	4	5	3
Warmth btw GM-C	5	5	3	5	6	4	4	5	5	3	3	5	1
Warmth btw M-GM	5	2	2	5	4	1	4	5	1	2	3	2	3
Child vs. parent centeredness	3	3	1	2	4	3	3	1	4	2	3	2	1
Disconnection	1	1	1	1	1	1	1	3	4	5	3	2	3
Shared focus	5	4	5	5	4	4	4	2	1	1	2	1	1
CBCL scores													
Mother reported													
Internalizing Problems	49	56	56	56	60*	61*	49	65*	—	65*	55	59	60*
Externalizing Problems	52	51	39	59	62*	67*	46	58	—	50	63*	48	61*
Total Problems	51	48	44	60*	61*	64*	44	62*	—	58	58	53	58
Grandmother reported													
Internalizing Problems	43	—	64*	70*	58	56	58	—	—	43	71*	69*	45
Externalizing Problems	39	—	51	74*	57	63*	62*	—	60*	43	77*	60*	54
Total Problems	38	—	57	76*	59	60*	60*	—	65*	41	74*	68*	48

Note. CFRS = Coparenting and Family Rating System; M = mother; C = child; GM = grandmother.
*Signifies clinically meaningful score on CBCL (Child Behavior Checklist).

Scores of 5: Mutually Supportive Coparenting Alliances

Adults in families receiving highest (Mutually Supportive) Coparenting Alliance scores shared leadership but allowed room for each adult to engage with the child. Five distinctively different families showed Mutually Supportive alliances. However, despite differences in tempo, style, and role distribution, in all cases both women consistently teamed together with the same common purpose, providing support and positive regard for the child.

The Harrison Family (Family 1)

Note: Pseudonyms are used to protect confidentiality. For this first family, we include CFRS codes in the text. Readers are referred to Table 12 *for ratings of subsequent families.* The Harrison child appeared to be a typically developing, happy and exuberant 5-year-old. His family's interaction was spirited and playful, with a relaxed tempo. Mother and grandmother cooperatively engaged with one another and with the child, supporting one another's directives to keep the boy on task as they joked and laughed (cooperation = 5). Neither woman behaved competitively (competition = 1; verbal sparring = 2), and both exhibited high and equal levels of investment when engaged with the child (mother–child/grandmother–child investment = 5/5; investment discrepancy = 0). Both women behaved warmly and affectionately with the child (mother–child/grandmother–child warmth = 5/5) and were positive and playful when engaged with one another (mother–grandmother warmth = 5). In short, the family was exceptionally cohesive, and judges observed no evidence of disconnection whatsoever (disconnection = 1). The threesome togetherness and joint attention was a distinguishing feature of the interaction (shared focus = 5).

The Gammons Family (Famiy 2)

Like the Harrisons, the Gammons family also appeared comfortable with physical demonstrations of affection. The child impressed as a typically developing, happy and low-key 3-year-old who, unlike the well-regulated and focused Harrison boy, showed occasional distractibility. However, each time she wandered off task, one of the two adults redirected her back as the other continued work on the task. Their teamwork in reintegrating the child back into the activity was noteworthy—as was their decision to take a "fun" break when the girl grew fatigued. Though shared focus was episodic rather than continuous, the impression of this family as a threesome was very powerful. Even when the girl took a back seat to the adults during the puzzle task, she signaled her continued connection by draping her arms across both women's shoulders as they worked. Warmth and cooperation were abundant, and conflict, competition, hierarchy, and disconnection altogether absent in the family.

The Marshall Family (Family 3)

In the Marshall family, the child was a restless, distractible 3-year-old. She spoke largely in two- to three-word utterances. In this family, one coparent

67

(the grandmother) typically acted first and assumed the lead. However, the mother accommodated to this stylistic difference and participated fully without ceding her own authority or leadership. The women complemented one another, working well together with no friction evident. They tag-teamed effectively when the child grew fatigued and protested. Their ability to work well together helped control the child and re-engage her when she wandered off task. Warmth among family members was high, and the coparents' success in re-engaging the child enabled moments of shared focus between the three of them. The adults also tracked the child, remaining patient with her even as she lost interest late in the session and became unfocused.

The Timmons Family (Family 4)

In the Timmons family, the child was a typically developing, well-regulated child who remained on task throughout. The adults showed co-leadership but a clear role distribution. The grandmother used physical contact, spoke gently to the child, and kissed her. Mother structured the tasks and was comfortable with grandmother's role. Mother–grandmother interactions were respectful, characterized by turn-taking, and always focused on the same aim. The women were also successful in creating threesome activities with the child's involvement.

The Cappell Family (Family 5)

The Cappell family was more subdued than any of the others. The child was an exceptionally obedient 5-year-old who showed signs of anxiety and hyper-vigilance. Both adults demonstrated task-oriented, directive styles. There was also very little mother-to-grandmother talk, but both women worked consistently to help the child without competing with one another or overwhelming him. Of note, the women's joint attention and support not only helped the child to stay on task but also to finish each task himself—a rare occurrence in the sample. The shared focus of this family was superb. Though no-nonsense at the beginning of the interaction while orienting the boy to the tasks, both adults did demonstrate affection and encouragement through touch and use of gentle voice tone as the session wore on.

Scores of 4: Led/Cooperative Alliances

Led/Cooperative families were distinguished by two features: (1) as with Mutually Supportive Families, there was clear teamwork between the two women, each showing sensitivity to the child's needs; and (2) one woman asserted more leadership or dominance than did the other *with the second showing occasional signs of wishing to be more involved.* Key, however, was that even when not in agreement, the duo succeeded in coordinating successfully.

The Mitchim Family (Family 6)

In the Mitchim family interaction, the girl was a typically developing 4-year-old, who engaged well with the task but showed episodic distractability and recalcitrance. Her mother issued most directions while her grandmother took a supportive role, was more Socratic and on several occasions appeared to have difficulty holding back. Yet overall the women maintained cooperative engagement and on two separate occasions when the girl's interest waned and she wandered off, the adults coordinated well to re-engage the girl and redirect her back to the tasks. Their collaborative effort restored a sustained, shared focus permitting successful task completion. Of note, while both women behaved warmly with the girl, they accomplished their coordinated coparenting in very business-like fashion, without any positive affective exchanges between them.

Scores of 3: Strained Coparenting Alliances

In strained coparenting alliances, a seemingly good foundation in the grandmother–mother relationship was accompanied by problematic elements. Two forms of dynamics were seen: (1) a generally positive and affectionate family interaction alternated with a "2 + 1" alliance with mother and child splitting off and excluding grandmother, signaling a potential cross-generational alliance, and (2) a strong and positive bond between the two adults did not translate into a sufficiently sensitive or effective scaffolding structure for the child.

Strained/Imbalanced Alliances: The Jacobs family (Family 7)

The Jacobs child was a high-energy, typically developing 4-year-old. His family was physically demonstrative and playful, chattering and making jokes. Mother's investment was unusually high, and she showed frequent physical contact with her son, who enjoyed staying in her lap. Both adults remained engaged with the boy throughout, but pursued different aims during the task. Grandmother sought to work through tasks in a structured fashion, while mother preferred simply to spend the time laughing and joking. She did episodically turn her focus to the tasks and the grandmother let the mother direct the child at these times. However, when the mother left the task to playfully commiserate with the child, the grandmother interrupted their interaction, prompting mother to make teasing remarks to the child. This was the point at which a 2 + 1 dynamic was clearest. The family did regroup—with grandmother ultimately joining the mother and boy in play, rather than persisting to complete the tasks.

The Davis Family (Family 8)

The Davis child was a typically developing 3-year-old. She demonstrated some anxiety and uncertainty. Her mother and grandmother showed an unusual degree of closeness, joking throughout the interaction. Grandmother maintained closer proximity interaction to the child but appeared to be holding back, perhaps so that mother could engage the child. But mother engaged verbally only from a distance and seemed not to know how to connect. The child hence did not get the support she sought; some of her signals even went unnoticed as the adults commiserated. So despite evidence of a positive bond between the adults, the child was poorly integrated in the threesome interaction and ultimately abandoned the task.

Scores of 2: Weak Coparenting Alliances

Inter-adult coordination and/or communication in families with Weak alliances were largely ineffective. Dynamics took two forms: (1) one coparent (in each case, mother) showed relative disconnection from the child and family while the second coparent (grandmother) showed sufficient leadership to permit the family to continue moving on task, and (2) a connection between the adults was negated by their incapacity to contain the child.

Weak/Disconnected Alliances: The Fischer Family (Family 9)

In the Fischer family, the child was a charming, very active 3-year-old who spoke in 1- and 2-word utterances and needed constant redirection. His mother acceded responsibility for guiding the child to grandmother, who remained highly involved with the boy, sought to help him complete the tasks, and responded to his signals in a gentle and accepting manner. The adults remained affectively disconnected from one another, showing neither positive nor negative engagement, and did not work in tandem to engage the boy. Despite her low level of warmth and investment, mother exhibited sporadic engagement with the boy, albeit typically only briefly and usually to scold him. Her high overall degree of disconnection appeared to make it difficult for the family to engage effectively as a triad, and they never achieved threesome moments together in which all had the same shared aim.

Weak/Disconnected Alliances: The Stabler Family (Family 10)

In the Stabler family, the recently-turned 6-year-old was small-for-age and behaved as a diminutive adult, participating in tasks in the same mature manner as did most study adults. Her mother made virtually no attempt to engage and at times even appeared internally preoccupied and disconnected altogether from activities going on in the session. Grandmother was very business-like with the child, providing sufficient structure and aid but only moderate warmth and attunement to the child's pace and signals. She did make overtures to the mother to draw her into the interaction so they might engage with the child and task together. Her efforts were ultimately unsuccessful, as the mother maintained her distance without arguing with the grandmother. Given mother's disconnection, the family was never able to achieve shared threesome focus at any point.

Weak/Ineffective Alliances: The Crest family (Family 11)

In the Crest family, the child was a typically developing, very recalcitrant 6-year-old. The adults showed clear hierarchy (grandmother structuring; mother relegated to a subsidiary role, to which she did not object) but unlike the other Weak families, there was regular conversation between the two women. In this family the child was the most disconnected member. Initially engaged, he lost interest and abandoned the assessment area. When mother observed that the task was too difficult for the boy, grandmother did not respond, continuing to work on the puzzle herself. Hence despite their connection with one another, the adults could not coordinate together as coparents to help contain the child.

Scores of 1: Harmful/Damaging Coparenting Alliances

In families demonstrating very problematic alliances, the adults were unable to collaborate to provide a positive learning environment, with coparenting behavior detrimental rather than helpful to the child. Problems came in two forms. One was an adult–adult rift marked by pervasive competition and conflict. The other involved absence of effective structuring by either woman, creating an impression of leaderless chaos.

Harmful-Competitive: The Jones Family (Family 12)

In the Jones family, the child was a socially adept but anxious 3-year-old who engaged in some role-reversal behavior. The adults vied for her attention, and both competition and verbal sparring were pronounced throughout. Mother showed some effort to collaborate with the highly invested grandmother, but grandmother did not reciprocate and actually thwarted some of the child's interactions with mother. The adults exchanged numerous snide remarks, and there was never a threesome, shared focus at any point in the session. The dissonance between mother and grandmother appeared to cow the child, who at one point even sought to have the adults make peace (give each other a "high five")—an overture both women rejected.

Harmful-Chaotic: The Hanson Family (Family 13)

In the Hanson family, the child was a typically developing, very oppositional 3-year-old. While there was none of the competition or verbal sparring seen in the Jones family, neither adult successfully controlled the girl's behavior. The cooperation they exhibited was superficial; while they parroted one another's reprimands, they never spoke directly to one another and remained impervious to the child's signaled needs. Grandmother exhibited more comfort admonishing the child, and showed no warmth toward the child. Maternal investment was higher, but warmth was also low. Given the adults' inability to control, structure, or calm the child, the threesome never played together with a shared focus.

DISCUSSION

From the standpoint of structural family theory, any child's chances in life would be bettered if all the central caregiving adults who play a formative role

71

in their life, co-resident or not, collaborated to co-create an environment that provided safety, structure, and responsive support to the developing child. From this vantage, findings from this investigation are uniquely important. Visiting families in their home environment just weeks after mothers' community re-entry following a jail stay, we were able to identify differences in the ways that mothers and grandmothers approached the task of working together to assist the child. Preliminary evidence indicated that differences in observed functioning within the coparenting interactions helped explain variability both in important child adjustment indicators and on other measures reflecting coparental quality, such as how the adults talked about their coparenting alliance and how closely in synch the two women were when reporting on child behavior problems. This new knowledge opens up important new avenues for both researchers and practitioners to understand resilience processes among children and families of incarcerated parents.

In contrast with images of recently incarcerated women struggling and adrift (Arditti & Few, 2006), the triadic interactions we observed, while varied, were refreshingly ordinary and largely devoid of observable pathology. Especially striking was the positive spirit and camaraderie of many interactions. Minuchin, Colapinto, and Minuchin (2007) have argued that most individuals who work with multirisk children, caregivers and families are too quick to generalize and to focus principally on deficits rather than on strengths. Seldom do researchers approach families in the manner of this investigation, allowing the data to lead wherever it may, rather than to conclusions of problems. However, we must also advise due caution so as not to make unwarranted generalizations on the bases of this sample and these data; because maternal incarcerations were 3- to 6-month jail terms (rather than longer term prison sentences), and because we sought families in which grandmothers had coparented the child prior to incarceration rather than just as an emergency measure, the extent to which family processes identified in this study will translate to other situations is not yet known.

Equally, we believe it possible that the insights into the everyday "normal family processes" of the families we worked with may have resulted from connections made with the mothers and grandmothers during the women's jail sentence, prior to release. Our study was enabled by a forward-looking jail system and set of administrators who concurred that women's adjustment upon community re-entry—and the adjustment of their young children to the mother's return—would potentially be promoted if the women maintained contact with their coparents and their children during their jail stay (Cecil, McHale, Strozier & Pietsch, 2008). The positive, initial connections jail personnel and study researchers made with mothers and grandmothers during the mother's jail term may have helped seed a more natural, ecologically valid family assessment during postrelease home visits.

Our data revealed that there is no one prototypical form of coparental adjustment in the unique sample we studied. In several families—the largest subgroup, in fact—we saw evidence of a positive bond between the two women as they worked collaboratively with the child. In other families, there was a clear hierarchy, but hierarchy itself did not signify whether women would be coparenting effectively. Rather, it was whether the women accommodated to the roles they played and remained sensitive to and involved in the aim of supporting the child. Overall, data mirrored in important ways family dynamics of samples where coparenting is most often evaluated. Families varied in the extent to which they actively collaborated, disagreed with one another, or engaged with the child in a balanced or less balanced fashion. The one major exception was the degree of maternal disconnection and disenfranchisement observed in family 10. Severe paternal disengagement is sometimes seen in the family interactions of clinical and sometimes even community samples, but severe *maternal* disengagement is relatively uncommon even in depressed samples. Further observational research is needed to determine whether parallels to this dynamic are ever seen in mother–grandmother kinship systems where there have been *no* been major traumatic upheavals.

Relatedly, given the very small sample, we cannot comment meaningfully on cultural differences among family systems. Both hierarchical and fully collaborative dynamics were found among both Caucasian and African American families. We do note that in no Caucasian family did mothers readily cede primary authority to grandmothers; in the two Caucasian families where grandmothers were more structuring than mothers, mothers participated actively. In the two African American families where grandmothers were more structuring than mothers, maternal participation was less intensive and mothers relinquished leadership to grandmothers. Although grandmaternal authority has been well-documented among low socioeconomic African American families (Burton, 1992), in the four Mutually Supportive African American families, leadership was balanced and shared, with no strong hierarchy in evidence. These important issues demand follow-up study in the future research literature.

Finally, we close with a few thoughts about how a better understanding of coparenting will benefit research and intervention in families of children of incarcerated parents. Recall the analyses linking measures of solidarity (high cooperation and shared focus, low disconnection and parenting discrepancies)—but not of conflict—to low Internalizing symptoms and positive child self-concept, and to the absence of an association between conflict and child Externalizing problems. One way to interpret this pattern of findings is to conclude that postrelease family observations are of principal use in detecting presence of mutual engagement and collaboration between coparents, critically important assets for protecting against anxiety and bolstering self-esteem, but that they are not as useful for understanding conflict or acting-out behavior.

We do believe that coparenting observations are well-suited to evaluate solidarity, but recommend that the absence of coparenting-externalizing problems connections not be over-interpreted. Children act up after mothers return from jail for many reasons. In three of the study families reporting significant child Externalizing issues (families 4–6), the coparenting alliance nonetheless impressed us as sound. Prospectively, we might speculate that the longer term trajectories of these three children would be more favorable than others with comparable behavior problems, precisely *because of* the strong coparenting alliance. The same might be predicted for the anxious child in family three whose grandmother reported significant Internalizing problems. The job of adults coparenting a traumatized child with Internalizing symptoms is no less daunting than working to aid an oppositional child. Good communication and collaboration between coparents, evident in the boy's family, will be crucial to help such children surmount anxiety and develop confidence. Despite his current symptomatology, we might be hopeful, given the capacity of the two women to work well together on his behalf.

Prospective studies of coparenting and child adjustment in high-risk samples are needed to test hypotheses framed in this manner. Such work will mark an important advance in the research agenda on resilience among children of incarcerated parents. Finally, we also see value in the assessment scheme offered here as a means of examining effects of coparenting and family interventions, to ascertain whether families having difficulties in their coparenting alliance are able to move toward more sustained, collaborative coparenting.

VI. A RANDOMIZED CONTROLLED TRIAL OF A PARENT MANAGEMENT TRAINING PROGRAM FOR INCARCERATED PARENTS: PROXIMAL IMPACTS

J. Mark Eddy, Charles R. Martinez Jr., and Bert Burraston

More than 680,000 parents of minor children are incarcerated in state prisons, accounting for 85% of all imprisoned parents in the United States (Maruschak, Glaze, & Mumola, 2010). These fathers and mothers are parents to 1.36 million children (West & Sabol, 2008). Prior to prison, almost half of incarcerated parents lived with at least one of their children, and more than half were the family's primary financial supporter. When their parents are behind bars, most children live with either another parent, or a close relative of the incarcerated parent, such as a grandmother, who may be the same parent who raised the incarcerated individual. About three-quarters of incarcerated parents report having had at least some contact with their children during their sentence, with up to 50% having weekly contact. Given these statistics, it is clear that many children of prisoners are living in situations that are directly impacted by the absence of a parent. Often these situations are quite challenging, and the present circumstances may be a continuation and expansion of difficulties that were present prior to incarceration (Travis & Waul, 2003).

Considering this context, it is not surprising that children of incarcerated parents have often been perceived to be at heightened risk for problems. Initially such concerns emerged from case studies and anecdotal reports, but over the past few decades, a variety of cross-sectional studies of incarcerated parents have found seemingly high rates of problems in their children (e.g., Baunach, 1985; Hunter, 1984; Myers et al., 1999). More recently, findings from longitudinal studies have become available (see Murray, 2010), and a meta-analysis found that the children of incarcerated parents were twice as likely as their peers to exhibit antisocial behavior problems, such as

---

Corresponding author: J. Mark Eddy, University of Washington, 1422 Oakway Rd., Eugene, OR 97401, email: jmarke@uw.edu

aggression, noncompliance, and stealing, even when other risk factors for these problems were considered (Murray et al., 2009).

Although actual data on the subject are sparse, such a finding implies that the children of incarcerated parents may also experience risk for eventual incarceration. Youth antisocial behavior is one of the most powerful predictors of adult adjustment problems, including criminal behavior (Kohlberg, Ricks, & Snarey, 1984; Lipsey & Derzon, 1998). Across numerous studies, 50–75% of youths who are arrested for delinquent acts or who meet criteria for a conduct disorder are arrested as adults (Harrington, Fudge, Rutter, Pickles, & Hill, 1991; McCord, 1991), and 40% meet formal psychiatric criteria for antisocial personality disorder (Harrington et al., 1991; Robins, 1966; Zoccolillo, Pickles, Quinton, & Rutter, 1992). Youth involved in criminal behavior during late childhood or early adolescence appear to be at particular risk for continuing such behaviors into adulthood and for incarceration (Gendreau, Little, & Goggin, 1996; Loeber, Stouthamer-Loeber, & Green, 1991; Moffitt, 1993; Patterson et al., 1991).

Notably, however, whereas the risk for a child of an incarcerated parent to exhibit antisocial behavior problems is elevated, it is not extreme. A doubling of risk does not suggest, for example, that most children of incarcerated parents are "destined" to become involved in crime or be incarcerated. As discussed in the papers throughout this volume, resilience in the face of difficult circumstances appears to be the rule, not the exception, and there are likely a variety of protective factors present in many families that mitigate the risks in the natural environment. For families with low levels of protective factors, it is conceivable that malleable factors might be developed or strengthened through intervention, and if successful, that a child of an incarcerated parent would not develop antisocial behavior patterns.

Parenting is one such malleable protective factor, and one that is of particular importance within the attachment theory framework (Poehlmann, 2010) that is at the center of most of the papers in this volume. Problematic parenting not only plays a role in attachment problems, but also is one of the driving social influences in models of the development of antisocial behavior (e.g., Reid, Patterson, & Snyder, 2002). Unfortunately, many incarcerated parents have childhood histories marked by inconsistent, neglectful, or abusive parenting, and they may have not had the opportunity to observe or develop positive parenting repertoires (Chipman, Olsen, Klein, Hart, & Robinson, 2000). Since most incarcerated parents will be released from prison, and many will function in some parental role after release (Mumola, 2000), the parenting skills of incarcerated parents may be important for reducing the numbers of incarcerated adults in the next generation.

Over the preceding decades, reasoning such as this has led to the proliferation of parenting programs for incarcerated parents. However, the scientific rigor of data on the efficacy of these programs has been weak. A review of interventions for mothers (Young & Smith, 2000) found only six studies of prison-based parenting programs that included a comparison group, and none used randomization. Five other comparison group studies existed (four of which were randomized), including three that focused on men (i.e., Bayse, Allgood, & Van Wyk, 1991; Block & Potthast, 1998; Harrison, 1997; Landreth & Lobaugh, 1998; Wilczak & Markstrom, 1999). Each of these studies used relatively small convenience samples. Most found that participants in the intervention group, relative to participants in a comparison group, had higher scores on at least one measure of positive parental attitudes or parenting knowledge immediately following the program. Few other variables were measured or impacted concurrently, and follow-up was rare (see also Loper & Novero, 2010). The programs studied ranged from relatively unscripted discussion groups to packaged interventions. Some programs had been developed or adapted specifically with the needs of the population of incarcerated parents in mind, but most had not. The descriptions of what was actually delivered to parents were often vague. Most importantly, none of the programs appeared to utilize the core elements of the type of parenting program that already had been demonstrated to impact child antisocial behavior in scientifically rigorous studies, namely Parent Management Training (PMT).

The evidence in support of PMT as an intervention for child antisocial behavior is compelling. In a review of 82 high-quality studies on the psychosocial treatment of conduct disordered children and adolescents (Brestan & Eyberg, 1998), the only interventions found to meet stringent research critieria for being "well-established" in terms of efficacy were two PMT programs (developed by Gerald R. Patterson and colleagues from the Oregon Social Learning Center; and by Carolyn Webster-Stratton from the University of Washington). In addition, PMT programs have been adapted for use beyond clinical settings, and a variety of evidence-based PMT prevention programs are now available (Reid et al., 2002).

The core elements for PMT are the "family management" skills of positive involvement, encouragement, noncoercive and nonaversive discipline, monitoring and supervision, and problem solving. Central to PMT programs are helping parents develop decision-making expertise concerning which skills to use and when, based on key factors such as the age and developmental stage of a child, his or her temperament, and the situation at hand. In short, PMT was a missing piece in the portfolio of research on parenting programs for incarcerated fathers and mothers, and the current study was designed to begin to address this gap.

Theory

PMT is grounded in social interaction learning theory (SLT; Patterson, Reid, & Dishion, 1992), a life course model of the development of antisocial behavior. The theory incorporates key findings on the development and maintenance of child antisocial and related deviant behaviors and of child competencies. SLT is grounded in several key findings. Longitudinal researchers have found that use of clear and consistent discipline techniques, close monitoring and supervision of the child, high rates of positive reinforcement, and secure, responsive child–adult attachment relationships are related to prosocial outcomes in childhood, adolescence, and adulthood (Fagot & Pears, 1996; Fisher, Ellis, & Chamberlain, 1999; Patterson, 1982). Further, research on the stability of antisocial behavior indicates that certain behaviors, like noncompliance and aggression, commonly begin at an early age in the context of parent– and sibling–child relationships when some or all of these parenting strategies and qualities are not present (Olweus, 1979; Patterson, Reid, & Dishion, 1992; Robins, 1978; Speltz, DeKlyen, & Greenberg,1999). Finally, early failures in discipline, continued child noncompliance, problematic attachment relationships, and low levels of prosocial skills appear to set the stage for reactions from teachers, peers, and parents that lead to the child being rejected and isolated (Patterson, 1982; Reid & Eddy, 1997). The cumulative effect of these experiences is the development of a coercive interaction style and an insecure attachment style. There is substantial evidence that once these are established, a child is at risk for problems across childhood and adolescence and into adulthood (Kazdin, 1987; Kerns, Klepac, & Cole, 1996; Schneider, Atkinson, & Tardif, 2001; Walker, Shinn, O'Neill, & Ramsey, 1987).

Throughout development, SLT emphasizes the interaction between the prior dispositions and learning of an individual and the environments to which he is exposed and to which he selects (Cairns & Cairns, 1994; Caspi & Elder, 1988; Hetherington & Baltes, 1988; Magnusson & Torestad, 1993; Rutter, 1989). At the heart of this approach (Bronfenbrenner, 1979, 1986) are individual interactions with the social environment. There has been increasing recognition that children are active agents in shaping their development and that parenting is done in conjunction with, rather than to, children (Kerr & Stattin, 2000; Kuczynski, Harach, & Bernardini, 1999; Maccoby & Martin, 1983). For example, sociable, emotionally regulated, and securely attached children are likely to exhibit a broad range of competencies later on, including sociability, popularity, perspective-taking skills, and a lack of social anxiety, even in the face of adversity (Bohlin, Hagekull, & Rydell, 2000; Cairns, Cairns, Xie, Leung, & Hearne, 1998; Englund, Levy, Hyson, & Sroufe, 2000; Sroufe, 1989).

The specific model of interest in the present study is based on SLT and focuses on the theoretical constructs most relevant to the incarcerated parent during and following prison (see Figure 2). Proximally, the intervention was intended to impact parent adjustment, specifically parent stress, depressed mood, and perception of playing an active role in the life of the child; the

78

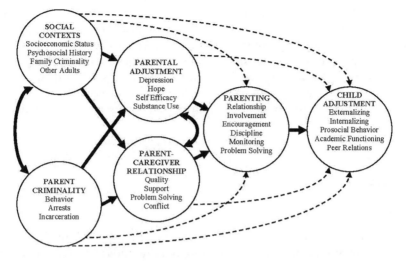

FIGURE 2.—Theoretical model.

parent–caregiver relationship, specifically in terms of ease of relationship with caregiver and feelings of closeness to caregiver; and parenting, specifically improving positive parent–child interactions. We hypothesize that improvements in all three of these areas during prison help set the foundation for the parent to gain a new sense of who they are as a parent and the life that they aspire to for their child, and to begin the construction of a new parenting role, however limited or expansive that may be, after release from prison.

The Parent Child Study

In this paper, we report on findings from the Parent Child Study, a randomized controlled trial that compared outcomes for incarcerated fathers and mothers assigned to PMT versus a "services as usual" control condition. The study was conducted in close collaboration with both the Oregon Department of Corrections (DOC) and a nonprofit service delivery agency with extensive experience working in the DOC, Pathfinders of Oregon. The PMT intervention, called Parenting Inside Out (PIO; Schiffman, Eddy, Martinez, Leve, & Newton, 2008) was designed for delivery to groups of incarcerated parents and was intended to provide parents with motivation, knowledge and skills relevant to their role in the prevention of the development of antisocial behavior and associated problem behaviors in their children. The development of the program is documented in Eddy et al. (2008). PIO is intended to be the first in a coordinated set of interventions that occur inside and outside of prisons with the purpose of improving outcomes for the children of incarcerated parents and their families. The current vision for this intervention set is described in Eddy, Kjellstrand, Martinez, and Newton (2010). The primary aim of the Parent Child Study was to examine the impact of PIO on incarcerated parents and their families. Here, we report on the most proximal outcomes for participants, after program completion and before release from prison, and specifically whether the intervention impacted indicators of three constructs in our theoretical model, parental adjustment, parent–caregiver relationship, and parenting.

METHOD

Study Design

Incarcerated parents were recruited from all 14 correctional institutions (i.e., prisons and work camps) in Oregon, but the study was conducted within four minimum or medium security level prisons (three for men, one for women) that were designated as "releasing institutions," where inmates were sent during the months prior to their release. Once an inmate expressed interest in participating in the study, potential study eligibility was determined (see criteria below), and if a participant who met all other eligibility criteria did not reside in a study prison, a transfer was requested. After a transfer was approved, to ensure a demographically diverse sample, women and minority participants were oversampled from the eligible pool, with goals of 50% women and 50% racial/ethnic minority participants. Participants were randomized into the PIO "intervention" condition or a services as usual "control" condition, and were then assessed prior to the start of the intervention, following the intervention, and at 6 and 12 months after release from prison. The study was approved by the federal Office of Human Research Protections and overseen by the Oregon Social Learning Center Institutional Review Board.

Eligibility and Recruitment

To be eligible for participation, an inmate was required to have (1) at least one minor child (with the target child age range from 3 to 11 years), (2) the legal right to contact the child, (3) some role in parenting the child in the past and an expectation of playing some such role in the future, (4) contact information for the caregiver of the child, (5) not committed either a crime against a child or any type of sex offense, (6) less than 9 months remaining before the end of his or her prison sentence, and (7) the DOC be willing to transfer him or her to a study institution. During the 3-year recruitment period, the study was advertised throughout the DOC through a variety of means, including advertisements in inmate newspapers, posters on bulletin boards, announcements during inmate club meetings, and special meetings about parenting and the study. To encourage minority participation, a bicultural, bilingual team of study staff members developed and employed recruitment strategies tailored for the major racial and ethnic groups represented in the corrections system. Inmates were invited to send a letter through prison mail if interested in the study. Of the 1,483 inmates who expressed interest in the study and who were screened, 453 were eligible. The most common reasons for ineligibility were no minor children and release dates that were more than 9 months away. Approximately 80% of eligible inmates consented to participate in the study. Overall participation rates were high for both fathers and mothers, but there was a significant difference ($p < .05$) in participation by sex, with 68% of eligible men and 92% of eligible women participating. The majority of men (51 out of 77) who did not participate did so because they did not want to transfer from their current institution to a study institution. If an inmate was interested in a transfer, almost all requests were granted. Reasons for not granting requests were not revealed to the study team, but were most likely due to security concerns. The DOC agreed to put transfers to other institutions on hold once an inmate enrolled in the study, and transfers of participants during the PIO program for a given cohort were rare.

Randomization

Randomization to condition was at the individual level, blocking on sex and on race and ethnicity. Since the intervention was delivered within specific prisons within which participants resided, and the program was delivered a limited number of times, randomization occurred within institution-based cohorts before the start of each new set of PIO sessions.

Sample

Participants ($N = 359$) included 161 incarcerated men (45%) and 198 incarcerated women (55%). In terms of race/ethnicity, 59% of participants were White, 13% African American, 11% multiracial, 8% Native American, and 8% Latino (vs. 75% White, 11% African American, 2% Native American, and 11% Latino in the DOC at large). Approximately 37% of participants had less than a high school education, 31% had a high school diploma or GED, and the remainder had at least some posthigh-school training or education (less than 1% had a college degree). On average, parents had three children. Most children were biological children, and the average child was 8 years old ($SD = 2.8$; range 1–15.6 years). In the month before incarceration, 34% of parents had lived with their children full-time, 9% part-time, 18% visited with their children at least once a week, 14% less than once a week, and the remainder had little or no contact. These values did not differ by sex of inmate. Men tended to have been sentenced for a person crime (61% vs. 40%, $p < .001$), to be serving longer sentences than women (2.2 years vs. 1.5 years, $p < .001$), and to have been in the custody of the DOC a greater number of times (1.7 vs. 1.4, $p < .001$). Women were more likely to have been older than men the first time they were arrested as an adult (23 years vs. 20 years, $p < .001$). Most parents had histories of drug and/or alcohol abuse or addiction (87% of men and 93% of women, $p < .05$), and many had histories of other mental health problems (27% of men and 45% of women, $p < .001$). Approximately 55% of participants had a parent and 53% had a sibling who had spent time in jail or prison. An even greater number had a parent (70%) or a sibling (61%) who had had problems with drugs or alcohol at some point in life. Intervention and control groups did not significantly differ on these variables.

Conditions

Intervention

PIO was delivered in a group format. Groups of approximately 15 participants met for 2½ hr sessions three times per week for 12 weeks, for a total of 90 hr of instruction delivered across 36 sessions. The meeting frequency and length of the program were set by the DOC, whose leadership desired an intensive, comprehensive, and research evidence-informed prison-based parenting program. PIO (Schiffmann et al., 2008) is an adaptation for incarcerated parents of the basic PMT program created by clinicians and research scientists from the Oregon Social Learning Center over the past 50 years (Reid et al., 2002). Based on focus groups with incarcerated parents and their families, observations of existing prison-based parenting classes, and interviews with prison-based parenting instructors around Oregon and the United States, the content and process of PMT was tailored to the incarcerated parent population. In addition to the core topics in PMT, added topics included communication and cooperation with the child's caregiver and other adults, thoughtful decision making around romantic partners postrelease, as well as topics found in existing prison parenting programs, such as child development, child health and safety, and positive parenting from prison through letter writing, phone calls, and prison visits. PIO sessions were designed to be engaging and interactive, and include brief presentations on parenting topics, video clips, extensive role plays, large and small group discussions, and class projects and skills building exercises conducted both inside and outside of sessions. In addition to group time, individual meetings occur between the parenting instructor, or "coach," and participants during the middle of the program to discuss unique family circumstances and find out if referrals for other services are needed. PIO was designed to be culturally respectful, but was not created to be culturally competent for issues within specific cultural groups. However, parents were referred to other appropriate groups, including religious services, within the prison to address cultural issues related to children and families, and were encouraged to participate in cultural activities of meaning and important to them and their families. The program was offered in English, but a culturally competent version of PIO was developed and delivered to Spanish speakers interested in participating in the study, and a separate pilot study was conducted with these participants (Eddy et al., 2013). Throughout PIO, participants were encouraged to discuss session information and activities with the caregivers of their children. Caregivers who requested class materials were sent handouts from the class. Caregivers were also encouraged to contact coaches if they had any questions or needed local referrals for services or other types of assistance. PIO classes were taught by coaches who were employees of Pathfinders of Oregon. Coaches were required to have experience working with parents and families, and a bachelor's degree and three years of clinical experience or an equivalent combination of education and experience. Experience teaching in a correctional setting and experience teaching parent education courses was preferred. Prior to teaching PIO, coaches participated in three days of PIO-focused training as well as additional training from the DOC and Pathfinders in procedures and protocols related to working in prison. New coaches observed experienced coaches teaching PIO, and then team taught PIO during their first few sessions. Coaches met or spoke on the phone weekly with their coach supervisor, and the coaching team met once per month with the coach supervisor and the principal investigator for group supervision and continuing education. Over the course of the study, 16 coaches taught PIO. Assisting coaches with classroom organization and activities were incarcerated parent assistants who had graduated from PIO.

Control

Historically, "services-as-usual" in terms of parenting interventions in each of the participating prisons had been a nonstandardized parenting program usually created by the person who delivered the program. Such programs were not offered on a consistent basis, and openings had typically been available for a relatively small number of inmates in a given year. Programs often focused on a discussion of how an inmate had been parented, rather than on how an inmate might actually parent his/her own child(ren), but varied widely in scope and approach. Few included elements of PMT. Most were lecture or discussion based, and offered few opportunities to practice new skills. Programs such as this continued in each prison during the course of the study. Participants assigned to the services-as-usual condition could not enroll in PIO, but like participants in the PIO condition, they had access to all other parenting programs or services for which they were eligible based on DOC requirements.

Assessment and Variables

Because of varying literacy levels, all interviews were conducted in person. Interviews were conducted preintervention, before the PIO program began in a given prison, and postintervention, after the completion of the program but before release from prison. Participants were compensated $30 for their time for participating in each interview. Interviews comprised nationally standardized questionnaires, in house questionnaires used on past studies with similar samples, and questions written for this specific study. Inmates were asked to identify one of his or her minor children, and interview questions at each assessment focused on that particular child and his or her current caregiver. Variables in the analyses were as follows. *Parent stress* was measured using 12 items from the 14 item Perceived Stress Scale (PSS; Cohen, Kamarck, & Mermelstein, 1983). Questions asked about feelings of stress in the past month such as "how often have you felt that you were unable to control the important things in your life" and "how often have you felt confident about your ability to handle your personal problems?" The internal reliability for the scale in this sample was $\alpha = .85$, similar to the reliability of the full scale in general population samples. *Parent depression* was measured with 20 items drawn from the Center for Epidemiological Studies Depression Scale (CES-D; Radloff, 1977). CES-D asks about the respondent's mood in the past week with questions such as "I felt depressed" and "I thought my life had been a failure." The internal reliability for the scale in this sample was the same as in past studies of the general population ($\alpha = .85$). *Likely to play a active role in child's life* was measured using one item regarding how likely an inmate thought it was that he or she would play an active role in their child's life six months after release from prison (1 "very unlikely" to 5 "very likely"; sample mean of 4.6, $SD = 0.9$). *Positive parent–child interaction* was a composite variable that was constructed from two sets of items. The first averaged scores from three items, each addressing parental perceptions about whether contact with his/her child had a positive, negative, or neutral influence on the child's behavior. The second averaged scores from four other items, each addressing parental perceptions of child behavior after parental contact (e.g., "after contact was the child happy"). The two scales were standardized and then averaged to compute an overall measure of positive parent–child interaction ($\alpha = .84$). *Ease of relationship with caregiver* was measured by standardizing and averaging 13 items relating to the parent–caregiver relationship (e.g., "how often does the parent and caregiver argue or disagree about the child," "how often does the parent and caregiver argue"). Reliability for the scale was acceptable ($\alpha = .88$). *Closeness to caregiver* was measured by standardizing and averaging nine items relating to the parent and caregiver relationship (e.g., "how much do you and the caregiver care about each other?" "how well do you understand each other?"). Reliability for this scale was also acceptable ($\alpha = .88$). *Family contact in prison* was measured by totaling the number of reported phone, letter, and in person contacts during the month prior to the preintervention interview; a transformation was used to normalize this variable (i.e., 1 plus the natural log). *Female* was a dummy variable, code 1 if the participant was female and 0 if male. *Condition* was also a dummy variable, coded 1 if the participant was in the intervention condition and 0 if in the control condition. *Age* was the age of the participant in years. All participants completed the interview before the PIO program began (preintervention), and 88% of participants completed the interview following the intervention and before release from prison (postintervention). Within a particular interview, variables were missing due to a variety of reasons, such as the late arrival of an inmate to an interview due to work duties, or the early termination of an interview due to a prison lock-down. In such cases, attempts were made to continue the interview, but were not always successful.

Analytic Strategy

Data were missing for some participants at the preintervention assessment point. We used the multiple imputation procedure in STATA statistical software (StataCorp, 2009) to impute missing independent (but not dependent, postintervention assessment) variables. For each missing value, we imputed 50 values and then used the mean of these values as the final imputed value (Bodner, 2008). Intervention participants were included in analyses regardless of whether or not they attended PIO sessions. Because participants were clustered by prison and by class (i.e., the PIO intervention was delivered to groups of 15 participants), we examined each outcome for significant nesting using STATA's multilevel mixed-effects procedure (Rabe-Hesketh & Skrondal, 2008). We found no significant nesting. Therefore, we used OLS linear regression analysis in STATA to test each outcome for a condition main effect, controlling for the baseline measure of the outcome as well as participant sex, age, and total family contact in prison. In a second model, we then tested for a condition by baseline interaction. Models were also run with race and ethnicity as controls, but no differences in outcomes were found.

RESULTS

Intervention Integrity and Fidelity

Of the 194 participants assigned to the intervention, 182 began the PIO program, with the remainder unable to enroll in a class due to a variety of reasons, such as unavailability due to work schedules. The average parent who started the program attended 24 of the 36 sessions, with 66% attending at least 20 classes. About one third of participants who started did not complete the program, including 36 who dropped out, 5 who were transferred by the DOC, 6 who were placed in disciplinary segregation, and 10 who discontinued due to other DOC administrative issues. Approximately 72% of women and 58% of men in the intervention condition were ultimately listed as officially "graduating" from PIO, a designation of meaning to the DOC that was determined by Pathfinders staff members and included a consideration both of how many classes an inmate attended and how positively involved they were in the class (e.g., completing homework, participating in class, appropriately behaved). The content of classroom sessions was tracked by the incarcerated parent assistants in each classroom. During an average class, 90% ($SD = 14\%$) of the curriculum content was taught. Classroom observations by the coach supervisor were conducted each month for each coach. On average, 5 classroom observations were conducted per coach. Coaches received an average score of 3.9 out of 5 (with 1 "below expectations" to 5 "exceeds expectations") on 32 questions related to appropriate teacher behaviors. Following an observation, a supervisor would meet with the coach, discuss his or her observations, and, if necessary, make a plan on how to improve teaching behaviors to be more congruent with the PIO model of intervention.

Consumer Satisfaction

Participants expressed strong satisfaction with PIO. On a scale of 1–5, with 5 indicating that a parent would "strongly recommend" PIO to other inmates, the average score was 4.5 and the median score was 5. Approximately 70% of parents rated the information they received in PIO as "quite" or "very" helpful. Over 90% of parents rated PIO as having a "positive" or "very positive" effect on them, and 95% rated the class as "somewhat" or "very" useful to them as parents.

Outcomes

The regression coefficients and significance levels for the models examined are listed in Table 13. Of most interest was whether intervention condition significantly impacted each outcome, and whether condition interacted with preintervention levels of the outcome. For three outcomes (i. e., parent stress, parent depressed mood, positive parent–child interaction), we found significant condition main effects, and for three outcomes (i.e., parent depressed mood, likely to play an active role, and ease of relationship with caregiver) we found significant baseline by condition interactions. Findings by outcome are described below.

86

TABLE 13

REGRESSION MODELS PREDICTING PROXIMAL OUTCOMES

	Parent Stress (n = 315)		Parent Depressed Mood (n = 261)		Parent Child Positive Interaction (n = 225)		Likely to Play Active Role (n = 309)		Closeness With Caregiver (n = 248)		Ease of Relationship With Caregiver (n = 246)	
	Model 1	Model 2	Model 1	Model 2	Model 1	Model 2	Model 1	Model 2	Model 1	Model 2	Model 1	Model 2
Constant	1.78**	1.77**	0.85**	0.86**	−0.92**	0.90**	2.75**	1.50**	0.07	0.06	−0.47**	−0.50**
Condition[a]	−0.13*	−0.13*	−0.11*	−0.12*	0.25*	0.26*	0.10	2.33**	0.02	0.03	0.07	0.07
Female[b]	0.02	0.03	0.11*	0.13**	−0.16	−0.18	0.03	0.01	0.08	0.07	0.22**	0.22**
Total family	−0.06	−0.05	−0.01	0.03	0.10	0.10	0.12*	0.11*	0.00	0.00	0.00	0.01
Contact	−0.01**	−0.01*	0.02	−0.01	0.03**	0.03**	0.01	.01	−0.00	−0.00	0.01	.01
Age	0.30**	0.32**	0.23**	0.32**	0.33**	0.42**	0.33**	0.58**	0.33**	0.42**	0.60**	0.72**
Baseline[c]		−0.06		−0.16**		−0.18		0.47**		−0.16		−0.24*
Baseline[c] by condition	0.25	0.25	0.28	0.30	0.23	0.24	0.06	0.08	0.19	0.19	0.38	0.39
Adjust R^2	22.1**	18.5**	20.9**	19.6**	14.3**	12.5**	4.8**	5.3**	12.2**	10.8**	30.4**	26.6**
	(5, 309)	(6, 308)	(5, 255)	(6, 254)	(5, 219)	(6, 218)	(5, 303)	(6, 302)	(5, 242)	(6, 241)	(5, 240)	(6, 239)

Notes.
$^*p < .05. ^{**}p < .01.$
[a]Control condition is the reference group.
[b]Males are the reference group.
[c]Baseline is preintervention measure for the given model (e.g., parent stress for parent stress model).

Parent Stress

There was a significant effect of condition on parent stress. Controlling for preintervention stress ratings, inmate gender and age, and total family contacts in prison, participants assigned to the intervention condition reported significantly less stress than control participants at the post-intervention assessment ($b = -.128$, $p = .03$). At the mean levels of the control variables, intervention participants were, on average, 8.8% lower on parental stress at postintervention than controls. Inmate age was negatively related to postintervention parent stress ($b = -.012$, $p < .01$) and preintervention stress was positively related ($b = .296$, $p < .01$). Neither inmate gender nor family contacts in prison were related to parental stress.

Parent Depressed Mood

There was a significant effect of condition on parent depressed mood. Controlling for preintervention mood, inmate gender and age, and total family contacts in prison, participants assigned to the intervention condition reported feeling significantly less depressed than control participants at the postintervention assessment ($b = -.112$, $p = .02$). At the mean levels of the control variables, on average, males in the intervention group were 7.4% lower on scores of depressed mood than males in the control group, while females in the intervention group were 7% lower than control females. Females reported significantly higher levels of depressed mood than males ($b = .110$, $p < .05$). The relation between preintervention and postintervention depressed mood scores was significant ($b = .225$, $p < .01$). Neither inmate age nor family contacts in prison were related to depressed mood.

In Model 2, the baseline by condition interaction was significant ($b = -.158$, $p = .002$), as was the main effect of condition ($b = -.119$, $p = .01$). Figure 3 depicts the relationship between preintervention depressed mood and condition for men. In the figure, the slope for the control group is much steeper than for the intervention group, and at very low levels of preintervention depressed mood (-2 to -1.5; 4.5% of sample), the control group fared the best. However, at the mean level and above for preintervention scores, participants in the intervention condition were significantly lower on depressed mood than the controls ($-.22$ and above; 50% of the sample). The percent difference between the intervention and control conditions varies by the preintervention score. At the mean preintervention score, intervention participants were 14% lower than control participants. The percent difference increases as preintervention score increase.

Positive Parent–Child Interaction

There was a significant intervention effect on positive parent–child interaction. Controlling for preintervention scores, inmate gender and age,

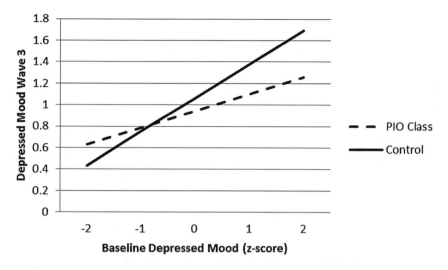

FIGURE 3.—Interaction between preintervention depressed mood and condition for men. *Note.* PIO = Parenting Inside Out.

and total family contacts in prison, participants assigned to the intervention condition reported significantly more positive interaction postintervention ($b = .254$, $p = .02$). At mean levels of the control variables, participants in the intervention group were 12.4% higher, on average, on positive parent–child interaction than controls. Inmate age was related to positive interaction ($b = .026$, $p < .01$) as was preintervention interaction ($b = .329$, $p < .01$). Neither inmate gender ($b = -.163$, $p = .14$) nor total family contacts in prison ($b = .100$, $p = .07$) were related.

Likely to Play an Active Role in the Child's Life

In Model 1, there was not a significant intervention main effect on likely to play an active role in the child's life. However, in Model 2, the preintervention by condition interaction was significant ($b = -.469$, $p = .01$) as was the main effect of condition ($b = 2.334$, $p = .01$). Figure 4 illustrates this interaction for males. The slope for the control group is much steeper than for the intervention group. Except for the very highest levels, participants assigned to the intervention condition rate themselves more likely to play an active role in their child's life following the completion of the PIO program. The difference between the intervention and control conditions varies by the preintervention score. At the lowest levels, intervention group participants were 180% higher than control group participants, but this gap decreased as the score increased.

89

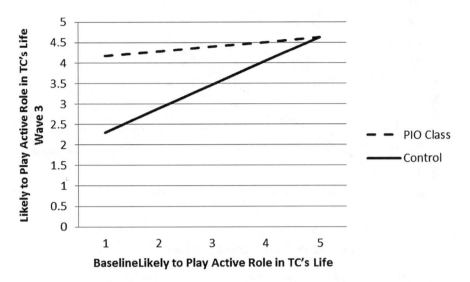

FIGURE 4.—Interaction between preintervention active role and condition for men. *Note.* PIO = Parenting Inside Out; TC = target child.

Closeness to Caregiver

There was not a significant condition effect in Model 1, nor a significant condition effect or baseline by condition interaction effect in Model 2. However, in Model 2, the baseline by condition interaction approached significance ($b = -.16$, $p = .08$). Again, the slope of the control group was much steeper than the slope for the intervention group. At low preintervention scores, intervention group participants reported higher scores than control group participants, and at high preintervention levels, there was a scant difference between the groups.

Ease of Relationship With Caregiver

In Model 1, there was not a significant effect of condition on ease of relationship with caregiver. However, in Model 2, the preintervention by condition interaction was significant ($b = -.24$, $p = .03$). As in the other baseline by condition interactions, the slope for the control group was much steeper than the slope for the intervention group, and thus the difference between the conditions varied by the preintervention score. At the lowest preintervention scores, intervention participants were 150% higher on scores than control participants. This gap decreased as the preintervention score increased until at the highest scores, the control group was higher.

90

DISCUSSION

The Parenting Inside Out program shows promise as one component in a preventive intervention strategy designed to improve outcomes and foster resilience processes within the growing population of children of incarcerated parents. The program expands on past efforts in prison-based parenting programs by incorporating content and process from a well-established, evidence-based intervention, PMT, designed specifically to target the development of child antisocial behavior. The rigorous evaluation of program outcomes described in this paper push the field beyond the small convenience samples and quasi-experimental studies of the past. Most parenting programs for incarcerated parents have not been studied in a manner that provides parents, practitioners, or policymakers the information they need to make good decisions about the value of the program. With this first look at outcomes from a relatively large scale randomized controlled trial conducted with a demographically diverse sample, high-quality information is now available to assist in consumer decision making.

On the basis of the findings presented here, Parenting Inside Out appears to have a significant impact on incarcerated parents while in prison in three areas of particular importance, parent adjustment, parent–caregiver relationships, and parenting. Some of these effects were main effects of the intervention, whereas others were interactions between the intervention and baseline levels of a given outcome. In the case of interactions, the intervention appeared to impact the parents who most needed the intervention, and had little impact on those in less need. This is the type of effect that would be expected from a preventive, rather than a clinical, intervention program.

Only a few parents in prison in the United States live with their children, and in all cases, the children are infants (see Byrne, 2010). Children require moment-to-moment, day-to-day parent–child interaction, and clearly, no incarcerated parent can provide such to children in the age group targeted in this study (ages 3–11 years). Even those fathers and mothers who do have regular contact with their children from prison do not see or speak with them often (Maruschak et al., 2010). Thus, the typical assumption underlying most parenting programs in the community, that parents will attend a group, learn some new ideas, and go home and try them out, does not fit for prison-based programs. Further, parents have been living in social conditions in prison, and sometimes for many years, that do not allow the practice of the characteristics of healthy relationships that are crucial to parent–child relationships, such as warmth, trust, and nurturance (see Travis & Waul, 2003). Secure attachments are not the norm in prison life.

Given this, it seems reasonable to hypothesize that the goals of a prison-based parenting program are different from the typical goals of a community-based program. Our primary goal was to help parents build a new vision for themselves as a parent, and to begin to make changes relevant for preparing a new, to-be-defined role as parent following release from prison. Our expected proximal impacts focused on the incarcerated parent because he or she was the person involved in the intervention under the highly constrained conditions of prison. Evaluating effects in parenting skills or even parenting knowledge when an individual is not actually parenting on a moment-to-moment basis is difficult and of potentially dubious value. In contrast, evaluating whether changes have taken place in the foundations for parenting, such as the relationship with a coparent and the relationship with the child seems quite reasonable and important. This was our focus here.

The argument can be made, and rightly so, that like past studies of parenting programs, this report focuses on only parent-reported points of view on self and relationship to others. This is not necessarily a weakness, however, when changes in parent-report are examined within the context of a randomized controlled trial. In the early days of the development of PMT, researchers recognized that regardless of observed changes, or lack thereof, in parent–child interactions, parents tended to report improvements from assessment point to assessment point (see Reid et al., 2002). In a randomized controlled design, the parents in the control group serve as a counter to this phenomenon. If more change is observed in the intervention group than the control group, perhaps some true change is actually occurring, and such appears to be the case here. Whether or not these changes are important in the child's life, however, remain to be seen.

In this regard, the next step in The Parent Child study is to examine whether the intervention had an impact on postrelease outcomes. Key here is whether parents in the intervention group continue to exhibit better adjustment than parents in the control group, and specifically in terms of areas that may lead to parent substance use and criminal behavior. Further, once a parent is on the outside, the full spectrum of parenting skills may now become relevant, depending on the role a parent plays in the child's life and whether or not he or she lives with the child or sees the child frequently. At this point, whether or not a parenting program like Parenting Inside Out has an impact on child behavior seems relevant.

Of course, to examine impacts such as these, an incarcerated parent and his or her family must be followed and assessed at repeated points across time. As other research teams have commented, this can be quite challenging (Eddy et al., 2001). Conducting a randomized controlled trial within a prison system and assessing parents in prison is one thing; following parents out into the community is another. In subsequent reports, we will present findings on our attempts to follow the parents after release and what happened, not only to them but to their children and the caregivers of their children.

On the basis of findings from this study to date, we continue to hold to our original ideas regarding the value of parenting programs in prison (Eddy et al., 2010). Such programs have the potential to impact incarcerated parents, and we continue to suspect that such impacts are an important part of making a difference in the lives of their children. However, we hypothesize that parenting programs are a necessary but not sufficient part of a comprehensive intervention for incarcerated parents and their children, and that without follow-up on the outside of prison, and without other interventions that provide parents and children with the supports they need to succeed, parenting programs for incarcerated parents are likely to have little long-term impact. Assisting former inmates in securing housing, finding a job, avoiding substances, engaging in positive interactions with family members, and staying away from situations that in the past had led to criminal behavior, including associations with deviant peers, are equally important considerations to parenting skill and knowledge development in prison and postprison parenting programs. Children may need such supports as well, especially as they reach adolescence and young adulthood.

VII. SCIENTIFIC AND PRACTICAL IMPLICATIONS

Julie Poehlmann

The new data presented in this volume further our understanding of individual, family, and peer-related processes that may protect children from some of the potential negative sequelae of parental incarceration. First, the studies suggest that emotional and social correlates of close interpersonal relationships, such as empathy and emotion regulation, are important for children of incarcerated parents, similar to children who experience other life stressors or risks. Second, two of the studies emphasize the importance of examining relationships and interactions beyond dyads in families affected by maternal incarceration, as intergenerational coparenting alliances and triadic family interactions may be important for children's well-being during and following a mother's incarceration, particularly when children are placed with their maternal grandmothers. Third, data presented in this volume suggest that current parental incarceration may be a particularly potent predictor of peer-related aggression in elementary school children. Fourth, results presented here contribute to our knowledge base regarding possible interventions to improve outcomes for children with incarcerated parents, including interventions delivered to incarcerated parents themselves. Fifth, children's age and development is an important consideration when examining risk and resilience processes in children of incarcerated parents. Finally, the studies have practical implications for how we conduct developmental and family research with children of incarcerated parents and their families. The studies in this volume break new ground in work with this population by using observational methods combined with child and parent self-reports, by assessing children in a diversity of contexts (e.g., home, school, summer camp), by recruiting participants across an entire correctional system, and by combining elements of various evidenced-based interventions.

Corresponding author: Julie Poehlmann, School of Human Ecology and Waisman Center, 1500 Highland Ave., University of Wisconsin, Madison, WI 53705, email: poehlmann@waisman.wisc.edu

Correlates of Close Interpersonal Relationships in Children With Incarcerated Parents

Several individual characteristics assessed in children of incarcerated parents, including empathy and emotion regulation, have been related to parent–child relationship processes in previous studies. Although there is a need for additional research with children of incarcerated parents to directly assess close interpersonal relationships, including parent–child interactions and attachment relationships, the work presented here furthers our understanding of how correlates of close relationships may serve a protective function for this high risk population.

Dallaire and Zeman's results showed that relative to most children, those experiencing a current parental incarceration evidenced low levels of empathy, according to a parent-report measure, although they did not differ from children experiencing parental separation for nonincarceration reasons. Importantly, their analyses indicated that empathic responding moderated the relation between current parental incarceration and children's peer-rated aggressive behavior; children whose parent was currently incarcerated who also had high levels of self-reported empathy were rated as less aggressive by their peers. When children have the capacity to show empathy, they may be protected from engaging in the worst forms of negative peer relations, especially in families of children experiencing current parental incarceration. These findings suggest that future research with children of incarcerated parents may do well to focus on facilitating empathy and positive relationships related to the development of empathy.

Another potential protective process explored in this volume involves children's emotion regulation in relation to teasing and bullying. In the Myers et al. study, children of incarcerated mothers attending a summer camp who were rated by adults as higher in emotion regulation were less likely to engage in bullying. Specifically, a one-unit change in emotional regulation resulted in a child being 5.8 times *less* likely to be classified as a bully. Emotion regulation is potentially another relationship-related process that may protect children from life stressors, including maternal incarceration. Future research should examine this possibility using larger samples of children with jailed or imprisoned mothers and fathers and including direct assessments of relationship factors (including attachments) that may promote such emotional regulation. Longitudinal data are particularly needed to answer questions regarding protective effects of relationships and relationship-related processes in children of incarcerated parents.

Attachment theory has been prominent in highlighting the importance of emerging emotion regulation and empathy in the context of dyadic relationships. As other scholars have noted, attachment theory can be useful in explaining the possible differential effects of maternal and paternal incarceration on children's development and in understanding the potential negative effects of parental incarceration on young children because of its emphasis on disrupted relationship processes and parent–child separation (Murray & Murray, 2010). Moreover, attachment theory can help guide interventions and research on resilience in children with incarcerated parents (Mariakev & Shaver, 2010). For example, it is possible to focus on the protective effects of a child's emerging attachment to a substitute caregiver when the parent is in jail or prison. However, there are several limitations to keep in mind when applying attachment theory (and other dyadic relationship theories) to families affected by parental incarceration. First, studies to date have not examined the quality of child–parent relationships prior to parental incarceration. Although it is possible that prolonged separation from an incarcerated parent can be highly stressful for children and represent a significant disruption in care, even if the prior relationship is anxious, it is also possible that some children never developed a focused attachment to the parent prior to incarceration. In the latter scenario, a "disrupted attachment" has not occurred, though the child may still have thoughts and feelings about an absent or unavailable parent that can affect the child's development (e.g., Shields, Ryan, & Cicchetti, 2001). Second, children's relationships to siblings and extended family members or fictive kin may be particularly important in families affected by parental incarceration; these relationships have rarely been examined in studies that have applied dyadic relationship theories to children of incarcerated parents. Third, a focus on dyadic relationship processes in families in which there are multiple (sometimes sequential and sometimes overlapping) caregivers for children may limit our understanding of key interactions that may contribute to resilience processes. A focus on broader family and cocaregiver dynamics, such as those highlighted in family systems models (Minuchin, 1974) and emotional security theory (Davies, Harold, Goeke-Morey, & Cummings, 2002), is important, particularly when multiple caregivers are simultaneously involved in a child's life. Thus, including assessments of relationships and family interactions beyond the dyad is warranted.

Relationships and Interactions Beyond the Dyad

Two of the studies presented in this volume highlight the importance of intergenerational relationships and triadic interactions for children of jailed and imprisoned mothers, especially when children are placed with their maternal grandmothers.

Based on a sample of imprisoned mothers, Loper and Novero Clarke examined whether child placement with either the maternal grandmother or another caregiver moderated the association between the mother's own early attachment experiences and the current cocaregiving alliance and mother–child contact. Analyses indicated a conditional effect based on where children were placed during the mother's imprisonment. When children were placed with the maternal grandmother, there was a significant association between imprisoned mothers' early recollected maternal warmth and their reports of a positive coparenting alliance with the child's caregiver, as well as higher levels of child–mother contact. However, these associations were not observed when children were placed with other caregivers. Results suggest potential benefits of placement of children with the maternal caregiver when there is a positive preexisting attachment between the imprisoned mother and caregiving grandmother. Understanding the implications of maternal attachment for child well-being may depend on where the child is placed during maternal imprisonment.

McHale et al. looked in-depth at intergenerational interactions in their observational study of children living with grandmothers and mothers following a maternal jail stay. The researchers acknowledge that for a sustained coparenting alliance to exist, enduring relationships need to tie together relevant family members, in this case the mother, child, and grandmother. McHale et al.'s research calls attention to the fact that among the families participating in their study, many of whom demonstrated strong coparenting alliances, all of the mothers had been part of their child's life for at least 12 of the baby's first 18 months of infancy, maximizing the likelihood that infant–mother attachment had already had a chance to develop, whatever its quality. They also note that grandmothers had been on the scene as coparents even prior to the mother's recent jail stay, enhancing the likelihood that a child–grandmother attachment also existed in the families studied. However, direct assessment of attachment was not reported, nor was stability in these attachments reported in the postjail period.

Most importantly, McHale et al. highlight the significance of a previously overlooked but centrally important unit of analysis in families affected by maternal incarceration: triadic family interactions. In most families in which mothers of young children serve jail or prison sentences, maternal grandmothers rather than fathers serve as the families' functional coparents. The dynamics of how these women work together to create a protective, supportive, and conflict-free environment for young children may help determine whether children successfully adjust to the challenges created by the circumstances and aftermath of the mother's criminal activity, although additional research with larger samples sizes is needed to examine coparenting dynamics and children's adjustment in families affected by parental incarceration.

Whereas many researchers and clinicians who are not familiar with systems perspectives or trained as family therapists may try to explain triangular dynamics on the basis of individual adult pathology or a history of problematic dyadic attachments, doing so can prevent recognition of the unique strengths that can be found in how the family has adapted as a multiple person unit. Given these considerations, an agenda designed to promote child and family resilience should focus not only on child–parent or child–caregiver dyadic attachments, but also on triangular and family-level coparenting interactions. Indeed, scholars studying children raised in families not affected by parental incarceration have found that family-level security is a key variable for children's well-being. This may also be true for children of incarcerated mothers and fathers, and it should be examined in future research with this population.

Current Versus Past Parental Incarceration

Research has often combined children who are currently experiencing the incarceration of a parent with those who experienced parental incarceration earlier in their lives or even multiple times in their lives (e.g., Murray et al., 2009, this volume). Although it is important to explore both short- and long-term sequelae of parental incarceration, it is also useful to delineate specific challenges that children experience based on whether the incarceration is current or occurred in the past.

By collecting data from a relatively large sample of elementary school children with diverse experiences, Dallaire and Zeman were able to distinguish between children who experienced past or current parental incarceration. Using parent-, child-, and peer-report measures in addition to observations of children during a behavioral task, the study examined children's empathic responding and aggressive peer relations. Children with a currently incarcerated parent were perceived as acting more aggressively than other children, including those who experienced a past parental incarceration. It is possible that children coping with a current parental incarceration are actively dealing with not only numerous risks in their environments, but also possible changes in caregivers (e.g., Poehlmann, 2005a), social stigma related to the parent's incarceration (e.g., Shlafer & Poehlmann, 2010), or issues related to negotiating contact with the incarcerated parent (Poehlmann et al., 2010).

For some children, however, the distinction between past and current parental incarceration may be blurry. Many children experience the incarceration of a parent several times during their childhood, as most felons who spend time in prison have a history of jail time (Glaze & Maruschak, 2008). When mothers are incarcerated, many children also experience the incarceration of their fathers, either at the same time or at a different time. Moreover, as McHale et al.'s observations indicate, coparenting can still be present and actively negotiated following a parent's release from jail. Parental incarceration at any time in the child's life may set a series of changes in motion, and these processes may continue even when the parent is released and reintegrated into family life. Although some family processes, stressors, and transitions are shared by families experiencing parent–child separation for other reasons (e.g., Poehlmann, Park et al., 2008), some processes are unique to families experiencing parental incarceration.

Intervention With the Children of Incarcerated Parents

By examining protective factors, the studies suggest that future intervention research might focus on relationship-related processes, including the development of empathy, emotion regulation, intergenerational relationships, coparenting interactions, and family-level security. Because many of these processes are influenced by parenting quality, it is also of critical importance to test the effects of parenting interventions on families affected by parental incarceration.

In their report, J. M. Eddy et al. examined the impact of an evidence-informed prison-based parenting intervention for incarcerated parents within the context of a randomized controlled trial. Relative to controls, intervention participants reported less stress and depressed mood, more positive parent–child interaction, and better relationships with children's caregivers immediately following the intervention. Thus, the intervention appears to have helped strengthen one of the most important systems related to resilience in children—the parenting system (Masten, 2001)—within the challenging context of parental incarceration. The findings from this study are an important first step in examining the impact of work done with parents inside the prison setting on children's family experiences on the outside. Additional research is needed to determine if the intervention directly impacts children's behavior and well-being, especially in the years following the parent's reintegration into community and family life.

Parental Incarceration and Developmental Considerations

The chapters in this volume presented data focusing on families with children who ranged in age from infancy to late adolescence. In their observations, McHale et al. examined coparenting of children in the preschool and kindergarten period (age 3–6 years), whereas other studies focused on peer relations during middle childhood and early adolescence (Dallaire and Zeman: 2nd through 5th grade; Myers et al.: 9–13 years of age). Two of the studies presented herein included a wide age range of children. In the Loper and Novero Clarke study, children's ages ranged from 18 months to 17.4 years in the maternal grandmother group and from 3 months to 17.6 years in the nonmaternal grandmother group, with a mean of 9 years for both groups. In the J. M. Eddy et al. study, children ranged in age from 1 to 15.6 years, but most were between 3 and 11 years of age. On the one hand, including a large age range potentially increases the study sample sizes and provides an opportunity to examine whether interventions or parental incarceration and resulting family processes have differential effects on child outcomes at different developmental periods. On the other hand, such a range imposes measurement constraints and limits the constructs that one can study in children.

Given the extremely wide age span of children included in the present volume, and the different constructs assessed in each study, are there any firm conclusions that can be made about developmentally mediated resilience processes in families affected by parental incarceration? Unfortunately the answer is "probably not." However, processes that appear salient at different ages can be highlighted as potentially contributing to resilience in children of incarcerated parents (see Poehlmann & Eddy, 2010). For example, triadic coparenting interactions during play or problem solving may be particularly salient for the prevention (or development) of behavior problems in preschool age children of incarcerated parents because of the likelihood of children's exposure to these interactions in the home and the importance of joint scaffolding and caregiver discipline at this age. As children's experiences expand beyond the home environment in elementary and middle school, peer relationships and interactions with other individuals (e.g., at school or at camp) become more salient. In these wider spheres of engagement, children often apply what they have learned at home (e.g., empathy, emotion regulation) to their new relationships and interactions, often leading to success or problematic interactions (e.g., social competence vs. bullying). Generalized feelings about coparenting alliances and intergenerational relationships may be important for children from the time that they are able to internally represent relationships throughout adolescence and into adulthood.

In discussing developmental considerations, it should also be noted that none of the studies in this volume focused specifically on infants or toddlers with incarcerated parents. Although the youngest child in the Loper and Novero Clarke study was an infant, data were collected from adults and did not focus on child characteristics or skills. Indeed, we probably understand the least about the development of very young children in families of incarcerated mothers and fathers, and this would be an important area for future research. Much of the research has focused on antisocial outcomes and other forms of child psychopathology that are not apparent until middle childhood or adolescence (Murray et al., 2009). In the future, it will be important to examine not only positive adaptations made by children at every age, including infants and young children, but also early skills that may serve protective functions in children of incarcerated parents as they grow older.

Methodological Advances and Future Research

The present volume presents several advances in research methodology for the study of children with incarcerated parents. First, the studies clearly identified the samples examined (e.g., current vs. past incarceration, maternal jail vs. prison stay). Second, in most of the studies, children were directly involved in data collection. Previous research with children of incarcerated parents has often relied on parental or caregiver report and not included children themselves. In the present volume, Dallaire and Zeman observed children's empathic behavior in a school setting and they used parent-, child-, and peer-reports to measure children's aggression. Myers et al. observed children in a summer camp setting and relied on mentor's reports of teasing behaviors. McHale et al. introduced a new methodology into the literature focusing on children with incarcerated parents—observed triadic interactions in the home following the mother's release from jail. J. M. Eddy et al. used a randomized controlled design for their intervention research, recruited incarcerated parents throughout an entire state, and accounted for missing data and clustering of participants in their analyses, all significant methodological advances for studies of interventions with incarcerated parents (see Loper & Novero, 2010, for a review of prior work).

Third, the studies focus on processes that contribute to individual or family resilience in children affected by parental incarceration. Most previous research in this area has documented only risks and negative outcomes (Murray et al., 2009). More high-quality research focused on child and family strengths is needed. Through such work, it is also critical to determine what processes can help children with incarcerated parents begin or maintain a positive developmental trajectory. Few prior studies have examined protective factors and processes for children of incarcerated parents, and thus, this volume significantly advances our understanding of such processes in this high-risk group.

Fourth, the scholars who contributed to this volume had to overcome numerous obstacles in designing and implementing the studies, including working with leaders, staff members, and parents within prisons, jails, schools, summer camps, and faith-based organizations. Scholars have known for a long time that working with families of individuals in the corrections system can be challenging for many reasons (B. A. Eddy et al., 2001); yet the investigators who designed and carried out the studies presented in this volume were able to overcome many methodological and pragmatic challenges. For example, it is difficult to achieve adequate sample sizes for studies focusing on children of incarcerated parents, and thus many studies in the literature have relied on small convenience samples. However, J. M. Eddy et al. were able to recruit a large sample of incarcerated parents, and they continue to follow this sample after release from prison and gather data from caregivers and children as well.

Taken together, these studies further our understanding of resilience processes in children of incarcerated parents and their families. Many processes documented herein involve interpersonal relationships, including those with parents, caregivers, peers, and multiple generations of family members. Interpersonal relationships are vital resources for children of incarcerated parents, and further research is needed not only focusing on the role such relationships play in their lives but also on how they can be strengthened. Other areas very much in need of high-quality research in

101

terms of resilience for children of incarcerated parents in the United States include the influences of culture, race, and ethnicity; impacts of racially and economically based discrimination and stigma on child and family functioning; change in children's developmental competencies over time and through different phases of parental incarceration (e.g., arrest, sentencing, incarceration, and reunification); and effects of incarceration-related events and protective processes on children during infancy and early childhood. Children of incarcerated parents rarely have been studied within the field of child development. Hopefully, this volume will stimulate new interest in work with this population that can guide future practices and policies relevant to children who find themselves dealing with challenging circumstances through no fault of their own.

REFERENCES

Aaron, L., & Dallaire, D. H. (2010). Parental incarceration and multiple risk experiences: Effects on family processes and children's delinquency. *Journal of Youth and Adolescence, 39*, 1471–1484. doi: 10.1007/s10964-009-9458-0

Abidin, R. R., & Brunner, J. F. (1995). Development of a parenting alliance inventory. *Journal of Clinical Child Psychology, 24*, 31–40. doi: 10.1207/s15374424jccp2401_4

Abidin, R. R., & Konold, T. (1999). *Parenting alliance measure: Professional manual.* Odessa, FL: Psychological Assessment Resources.

Ablow, J. C., & Measelle, J. R. (1993). *Berkeley puppet interview: Administration and scoring system manuals.* Berkeley: University of California.

Achenbach, T. M., McConaughy, S. H., & Howell, C. T. (1987). Child/adolescent behavioral and emotional problems: Implications of cross-informant correlations for situational specificity. *Psychology Bulletin, 101*, 213–232.

Achenbach, T. M., & Ruffle, T. M. (2000). The child behavior checklist and related forms for assessing behavioral/emotional problems and competencies. *Pediatrics in Review, 21*, 265–271. doi: 10.1542/pir.21-8-265

Aiken, L. S., & West, S. G. (1991). *Multiple regression: Testing and interpreting interactions.* Newbury Park, CA: SAGE.

Arditti, J. A. (2003). Locked doors and glass walls: Family visiting at a local jail. *Journal of Loss and Trauma, 8*, 115–138. doi: 10.1080/15325020305864

Arditti, J. A., & Few, A. (2008). Maternal distress and women's reentry into family and community life. *Family Process, 47*, 303–321. doi: 10.1111/j.1545-5300.2008.00255.x

Arditti, J. A., & Few, A. L. (2006). Mothers' reentry into family life after incarceration. *Criminal Justice Policy Review, 17*, 103–123. doi: 10.1177/0887403405282450

Arditti, J. A., Lambert-Shute, J., & Joest, K. (2003). Saturday morning at the jail: Implications of incarceration for families and children. *Family Relations, 52*, 195–204.

Austin, J., & Irwin, J. (2001). *It's about time: America's imprisonment binge.* Belmont, CA: Wadsworth Publishing Co.

Baker, J., McHale, J., Strozier, A., & Cecil, D. (2010). Mother–grandmother coparenting relationships in families with incarcerated mothers: A pilot investigation. *Family Process, 49*, 165–184. doi: 10.1111/j.1545-5300.2010.01316.x

Barnett, M. A., Barlett, N. D., Livengood, J. L., Murphy, D. L., & Brewton, K. E. (2010). Factors associated with children's anticipated responses to ambiguous teases. *The Journal of Genetic Psychology, 171*, 54–72.

Barnett, M. A., Burns, S. R., Sanborn, F. W., Bartel, J. S., & Wilds, S. J. (2004). Antisocial and prosocial teasing among children: Perceptions and individual differences. *Social Development, 13*, 292–310. doi: 10.1111/j.1467-9507.2004.000268.x

Baunach, P. J. (1985). *Mothers in prison.* New Brunswick, NJ: Rutgers University Press.

Bayse, D. J., Allgood, S. M., & Van Wyk, P. H. (1991). Family life education: An effective tool for prisoner rehabilitation. *Family Relations*, **40**, 254–257. doi: 10.2307/585008

Bell, R. Q. (1968). A reinterpretation of the direction of effects in studies of socialization. *Psychological Review*, **75**, 81–95.

Belsky, J., & Fearon, R. M. P. (2002). Infant–mother attachment security, contextual risk, and early development: A moderational analysis. *Development and Psychopathology*, **14**, 293–310. doi: 10.1017/S0954579402002067

Block, K. J., & Potthast, M. J. (1998). Girl scouts beyond bars: Facilitating parent–child contact in correctional setting. *Child Welfare*, **77**(5), 561–578

Bodner, T. (2008). What improves with increased missing data imputations? *Structural Equation Modeling*, **15**, 651–675. doi: 10.1080/10705510802339072

Bohlin, G., Hagekull, B., & Rydell, A.-M. (2000). Attachment and social functioning: A longitudinal study from infancy to middle childhood. *Social Development*, **9**(1), 24–39. doi: 10.1111/1467-9507.00109

Bornstein, M. H. (2005). Positive parenting and positive development in children. In R. Lerner, F. Jacobs, & D. Wertlieb (Eds.), *Applied developmental science: An advanced textbook* (pp. 155–178). Thousand Oaks, CA: SAGE.

Bouthillier, D., Julien, D., Dube, M., Belanger, I., & Hamelin, M. (2002). Predictive validity of adult attachment measures in relation to emotion regulation behaviors in marital interactions. *Journal of Adult Development*, **9**, 291–305. doi: 10.1023/A:1020291011587

Bowlby, J. (1973). *Attachment and loss, volume 2. Separation: Anxiety and anger*. New York: Basic Books.

Brendgen, M., Vitaro, F., & Bukowski, W. M. (2000). Stability and variability of adolescents' affiliation with delinquent friends: Predictors and consequences. *Social Development*, **9**, 205–225. doi: 10.1111/1467-9507.00120

Brestan, E. V., & Eyberg, S. M. (1998). Effective psychosocial treatments of conduct-disordered children and adolescents: 29 years, 82 studies, and 5,272 kids. *Journal of Clinical Child Psychology*, **27**, 180–189. doi: 10.1207/s15374424jccp2702_5

Brody, G. H., Flor, D. L., & Neubaum, E. (1998). Coparenting processes and child competence among rural African American families. In M. Lewis & C. Feiring (Eds.), *Families, risk, and competence* (pp. 227–243). Mahwah, NJ: Erlbaum.

Bryant, B. K. (1982). An index of empathy for children and adolescents. *Child Development*, **53**, 413–425. doi: 10.1111/j.1467-8624.1982.tb01331.x

Bureau of Justice Statistics. (2010). Terms and definitions. Retrieved January 2, 2010, from http://bjs.ojp.usdoj.gov/index.cfm?ty=tda

Burton, L. M. (1992). Black grandparents rearing children of drug-addicted parents: Stressors, outcomes, and social service needs. *The Gerontologist*, **32**, 744–751.

Byrne, M. W. (2010). Interventions: within prison nurseries. In J. M. Eddy & J. Poehlmann (Eds.), *Children of incarcerated parents: A handbook for researchers and practitioners* (pp. 161–188). Washington, DC: Urban Institute Press.

Cairns, R. B., & Cairns, B. D. (1994). *Lifelines and risks*. New York: Cambridge University Press.

Cairns, R. B., Cairns, B. D., Xie, H., Leung, M.-C., & Hearne, S. (1998). Paths across generations: Academic competence and aggressive behaviors in young mothers and their children. *Developmental Psychology*, **34**(6), 1162–1174. doi: 10.1037//0012-1649.34.6.1162

Caldera, Y. M., & Lindsey, E. W. (2006). Coparenting, mother–infant interaction, and infant–parent attachment relationships in two-parent families. *Journal of Family Psychology*, **20**, 275–283. doi: 10.1037/0893-3200.20.2.275

Calkins, S. D., & Hill, A. (2007). Caregiver influences on emerging emotion regulation: Biological and environmental transactions in early development. In J. J. Gross (Ed.), *Handbook of Emotion Regulation* (pp. 229–248). New York: Guilford Press.

Calkins, S. D., Smith, C. L., Gill, K. L., & Johnson, M. C. (1998). Maternal interactive style across contexts: Relations to emotional, behavioral, and physiological regulation during toddlerhood. *Social Development*, **7**, 350–369. doi: 10.1111/1467-9507.00072

Caspi, A., & Elder, G. H. (1988). Childhood precursors of the life course: Early personality and life disorganization. In E. M. Hetherington, R. M. Lerner, & M. Perlmutter (Eds.), *Child development in life-span perspective* (pp. 115–142). Hillsdale, NJ: Erlbaum.

Cecil, D. K., McHale, J., Strozier, A., & Pietsch, J. (2008). Female inmates, family caregivers, and young children's adjustment: A research agenda and implications for corrections programming. *Journal of Criminal Justice*, **36**, 513–521. doi: 10.1016/j.jcrimjus.2008.09.002

Chipman, S., Olsen, S., Klein, S., Hart, C., & Robinson, C. (2000). Differences in retrospective perceptions of parenting of male and female inmates and non-inmates. *Family Relations*, **49** (1), 5–11. doi: 10.1111/j.1741-3729.2000.00005.x

Cho, R. M. (2009). The impact of maternal imprisonment on children's probability of grade retention: Results from Chicago public schools. *Journal of Urban Economics*, **65**, 11–23. doi: 10.1016/j.jue.2008.09.004

Chyung, Y., & Lee, J. (2008). Intimate partner acceptance, remembered parental acceptance in childhood, and psychological adjustment among Korean college students in ongoing attachment relationships. *Cross-Cultural Research*, **42**, 77–86. doi: 10.1177/1069397107309857

Cohen, D., & Strayer, J. (1996). Empathy in conduct-disordered and comparison youth. *Developmental Psychology*, **32**, 988–998. doi: 10.1037//0012-1649.32.6.988

Cohen, S., Kamarck, T., & Mermelstein, R. (1983). A global measure of perceived stress. *Journal of Health and Social Behavior*, **24**, 385–396. doi: 10.2307/2136404

Collins, N. L., & Feeney, B. C. (2004). Working models of attachment shape perceptions of social support: Evidence from the experimental and observational studies. *Journal of Personality and Social Psychology*, **87**, 363–383. doi: 10.1037/0022-3514.87.3.363

Compas, B. E. (1987). Coping with stress during childhood and adolescence. *Psychological Bulletin*, **101**, 393–403.

Cowan, C. P., & Cowan, P. A. (1992). *When partners become parents: The big life change for couples.* New York: Basic Books.

Crick, N. R., & Dodge, K. A. (1994). A review and reformulation of social information processing mechanisms in children's social adjustment. *Psychological Bulletin*, **115**, 74–101.

Crowell, J. A., Treboux, D., Gao, Y., Fyffe, C., Pan, H., & Waters, E. (2002). Assessing secure base behavior in adulthood: Development of a measure, links to adult attachment representations and relations to couples' communication and reports of relationships. *Developmental Psychology*, **38**, 679–693. doi: 10.1037/0012-1649.38.5.679

Dallaire, D. (2007a). Children with incarcerated mothers: Developmental outcomes, special challenges and recommendations. *Journal of Applied Developmental Psychology*, **28**, 15–24. doi: 10.1016/j.appdev.2006.10.003

Dallaire, D. H. (2007b). Incarcerated mothers and fathers: A comparison of risks for children and families. *Family Relations*, **56**, 440–453. doi: 10.1111/j.1741-3729.2007.00472.x

Dallaire, D. H., & Weinraub, M. (2007). Infant–mother attachment security and children's anxiety and aggression at first grade. *Journal of Applied Developmental Psychology*, **28**, 477–492. doi: 10.1016/j.appdev.2007.06.005

Dallaire, D. H., & Wilson, L. (2010). The impact of exposure to parental criminal activity, arrest, and sentencing on children's academic competence and externalizing behavior. *Journal of Child and Family Studies*, **19**, 404–418. doi: 10.1007/s10826-009-9311-9

Davies, P. T., Harold, G. T., Goeke-Morey, M. C., & Cummings, E. M. (2002). Child emotional security and interparental conflict. *Monographs of the Society for Research in Child Development*, **67**, Serial No. 270, pp. 1–127. doi: 10.1111/1540-5834.00207

de Kemp, R. A. T., Overbeek, G., de Wied, M., Engels, R. C. M. E., & Scholte, R. H. J. (2007). Early adolescent empathy, parental support, and antisocial behavior. *The Journal of Genetic Psychology: Research and Theory on Human Development*, **168**, 5–18. doi: 10.3200/GNTP.168.1.5-18

de Wied, M., Maas, C., van Goozen, S., Vermande, M., Engels, R., Meeus, W., et al. (2007). Bryant's empathy index: A closer examination of its internal structure. *European Journal of Psychological Assessment*, **23**, 99–104. doi: 10.1027/1015-5759.23.2.99

de Wolff, M., & van Ijzendoorn, M. H. (1997). Sensitivity and attachment: A meta-analysis on parental antecedents of infant attachment. *Child Development*, **68**, 571–591.

Denham, S. (1998). *Emotional development in young children*. New York: Guilford Press.

Dodge, K. A., Lansford, J. E., Burks, V. S., Bates, J. E., Pettit, G. S., Fontaine, R., et al. (2003). Peer rejection and social information-processing factors in the development of aggressive behavior problems in children. *Child Development*, **74**, 374–393.

Durbin, C. E. (2010). Validity of young children's self-reports of their emotion in response to structured laboratory tasks. *Emotion*, **4**, 519–535. doi: 10.1037/a0019008

Eddy, B. A., Powell, M. J., Szuba, M. H., McCool, M. L., & Kuntz, S. (2001). Challenges in research with incarcerated parents and importance in violence prevention. *American Journal of Preventive Medicine*, **20** (Suppl 1), 56–62. doi: 10.1016/S0749-3797(00)00273-7

Eddy, J. M., Kjellstrand, J., Martinez, C. R., Jr., & Newton, R. (2010). Theory-based multimodal parenting intervention for incarcerated parents and their children. In J. M. Eddy & J. Poehlmann (Eds.), *Children of incarcerated parents: A handbook for researchers and practitioners* (pp. 237–264). Washington, DC: Urban Institute Press.

Eddy, J. M., Martinez, C. R., Jr., Schiffmann, T., Ollade, R., Mujica, A., & Herrera, D. (2013). A culturally competent parent management training program for Spanish speaking incarcerated parents: A pilot study (submitted for publication).

Eddy, J. M., Martinez, C. R., Jr., Schiffmann, T., Newton, R., Olin, L., Leve, L., et al. (2008). Development of a multisystemic parent management training intervention for incarcerated parents, their children and families. *Clinical Psychologist*, **12**(3), 86–98. doi: 10.1080/13284200802495461

Eddy, J. M., & Poehlmann, J. (Eds.). (2010). *Children of incarcerated parents: A handbook for researchers and practitioners*. Washington, DC: Urban Institute Press.

Eder, D. (1991). The role of teasing in adolescent peer group culture. *Sociological Studies of Child Development*, **4**, 181–197.

Eisenberg, N., Cumberland, A., & Spinrad, T. L. (1998). Parental socialization of emotion. *Psychological Inquiry*, **9**, 241–273. doi: 10.1207/s15327965pli0904_1

Eisenberg, N., Cumberland, A., Spinrad, T. L., Fabes, R. A., Shepard, S. A., Reiser, M., et al. (2001). The relations of regulation and emotionality to children's externalizing and internalizing problem behavior. *Child Development*, **72**, 1112–1134. doi: 10.1111/1467-8624.00337

Englund, M. M., Levy, A. K., Hyson, D. M., & Sroufe, L. A. (2000). Adolescent social competence: Effectiveness in a group setting. *Child Development*, **71**(4), 1049–1060. doi: 10.1111/1467-8624.00208

Evans, G. W., Gonnella, C., Marcynyszyn, L. A., Gentile, L., & Salpekar, N. (2005). The role of chaos in poverty and children's socioemotional adjustment. *Psychological Science*, **16**, 560–565. doi: 10.1111/j.0956-7976.2005.01575.x

Fagot, B. I., & Pears, K. C. (1996). Changes in attachment during the third year: Consequences and predictions. *Development and Psychopathology*, **8**, 325–344. doi: 10.1017/S0954579400007124

Finger, B., Hans, S. L., Berstein, V. J., & Cox, S. M. (2009). Parent relationship quality and infant–mother attachment. *Attachment and Human Development*, **11**, 285–306. doi: 10.1080/14616730902814960

Fisher, P. A., Ellis, B. H., & Chamberlain, P. (1999). Early intervention foster care: A model for preventing risk in young children who have been maltreated. *Children Services: Social Policy, Research, and Practice*, **2**(3), 159–182.

Fivaz-Depeursinge, E., & Corboz-Warnery, A. (1999). *The primary triangle: A developmental systems view of mothers, fathers, and infants*. New York: Basic Books.

Frosch, C. A., Mangelsdorf, S. C., & McHale, J. L. (2000). Marital behavior and the security of preschool-parent attachment relationships. *Journal of Family Psychology*, **14**, 144–161. doi: 10.1037//0893-32O0.14.U44

Garbarino, J. (1990). The human ecology of early risk. In S. J. Meisels & J. P. Shonkoff (Eds.), *Handbook of early childhood intervention* (pp. 78–96). New York: Cambridge University Press.

Gendreau, P., Little, T., & Goggin, C. (1996). A meta-analysis of the predictors of adult offender recidivism: What works? *Criminology*, **34**, 575–606.

Glaze, L. E., & Maruschak, L. M. (2008). *Special report: Parents in prison and their minor children*. Washington, DC: U.S. Department of Justice, Bureau of Justice Statistics.

Grusec, J. E., & Davidov, M. (2010). Integrating different perspectives on socialization theory and research: A domain-specific approach. *Child Development*, **81**, 687–709. doi: 10.1111/j.1467-8624.2010.01426.x

Hagen, K. A., & Myers, B. J. (2003). The effect of secrecy and social support on behavioral problems in children of incarcerated women. *Journal of Child and Family Studies*, **12**, 229–242. doi: 10.1023/A:1022866917415

Hagen, K. A., Myers, B. J., & Mackintosh, V. H. (2005). Hope, social support, and behavioral problems in at-risk children. *American Journal of Orthopsychiatry*, **75**, 211–219. doi: 10.1037/0002-9432.75.2.211

Hanlon, T. E., Blatchley, R. J., Bennett-Sears, T., O'Grady, K. E., & Callaman, J. M. (2005). Vulnerability of children of incarcerated addict mothers: Implications for preventive intervention. *Children and Youth Services Review*, **27**, 67–84. doi: 10.1037/0002-9432.75.2.211

Hanlon, T. E., Carswell, S. B., & Rose, M. (2007). Research on the caretaking of children of incarcerated parents: Findings and their service delivery implications. *Children and Youth Services Review*, **29**, 348–362. doi: 10.1016/j.childyouth.2006.09.001

Harrington, R., Fudge, H., Rutter, M., Pickles, A., & Hill, J. (1991). Adult outcome of childhood and adolescent depression: I. Links with antisocial disorder. *Journal of the American Academy of Child and Adolescent Psychiatry*, **30**, 434–439.

Harrison, K. (1997). Parental training for incarcerated fathers: Effects on attitudes, self-esteem, and children's self perceptions. *Journal of Social Psychology*, **137**(5), 588–593. doi: 10.1080/00224549709595480

Hayslip, B., & Kaminski, P. L. (2005). Grandparents raising their grandchildren: a review of the literature and suggestions for practice. *Gerontologist*, **45**, 262–269. doi: 10.1093/geront/45.2.262

Hetherington, E. M., & Baltes, P. B. (1988). Child psychology and life-span development. In E. M. Hetherington, & R. M. Lerner (Eds.), *Child development in life-span perspective* (pp. 1–19). Hillsdale, NJ: Erlbaum.

Hodges, E. V. E., & Perry, D. G. (1999). Personal and interpersonal antecedents and consequences of victimization by peers. *Journal of Personality and Social Psychology*, **76**, 677–685. doi: 10.1037//0022-3514.76.4.677

Holmqvist, R. (2008). Psychopathy and affect consciousness in young criminal offenders. *Journal of Interpersonal Violence*, **23**, 209–224. doi: 10.1177/0886260507309341

Houck, K. D. F., & Loper, A. B. (2002). The relationship of parenting stress to adjustment among mothers in prison. *American Journal of Orthopsychiatry*, **72**, 548–558. doi: 10.1037//0002-9432.72.4.548 http://www.sentencingproject.org/template/page.cfm?id=128

Hourigan, S. E., Goodman, K. L., & Southam-Gerow, M. A. (2011). Discrepancies in parents' and children's reports of child emotion regulation. *Journal of Experimental Child Psychology*, **110**, 198–212.

Huebner, B. M., & Gustafson, R. (2007). The effect of maternal incarceration on adult offspring involvement in the criminal justice system. *Journal of Criminal Justice*, **35**, 283–296. doi: 10.1016/j.jcrimjus.2007.03.005

Hunter, S. M. (1984). The relationship between women offenders and their children. *Dissertation Abstracts International*, **45**(8), 1–286.

Izard, C. E., King, K. A., Trentacosta, C. J., Laurenceau, J. P., Morgan, J. K., & Krauthamer-Ewing, E. S. (2008). Accelerating the development of emotion competence in Head Start children. *Development and Psychopathology*, **20**, 369–397. doi: 10.1017/S0954579408000175

Johnson, E. I., & Waldfogel, J. (2004). Children of incarcerated parents: Multiple risks and children's living arrangements. In M. Pattillo, D. Weiman, & B. Western (Eds.), *Imprisoning America: The social effects of mass incarceration* (pp. 97–131). New York: Russell Sage Foundation.

Jolliffe, D., & Farrington, D. P. (2004). Empathy and offending: A systematic review and meta analysis. *Aggression & Violent Behavior*, **9**, 441–476. doi: 10.1016/j.avb.2003.03.001

Joo, B. (2008). *The relationship between past experiences of child abuse and current parenting practices among incarcerated women.* Unpublished doctoral dissertation, University of Virginia, Charlottesville, VA.

Kazdin, A. E. (1987). Treatment of antisocial behavior in children: Current status and future directions. *Psychological Bulletin*, **102**, 187–203. doi: 10.1037//0033-2909.102.2.187

Keltner, D., Capps, L., Kring, A. M., Young, R. C., & Heerey, E. A. (2001). Just teasing: A conceptual analysis and empirical review. *Psychological Bulletin*, **127**, 229–248. doi: 10.1037//0033-2909.127.2.229

Kemper, K. J., & Rivara, F. P. (1993). Parents in jail. *Pediatrics*, **92**, 261–264.

Kerns, K. A. (2008). Attachment in middle childhood. In J. Cassidy & P. R. Shaver (Eds.), *Handbook of attachment: Theory, research, and clinical applications* (2nd ed., pp. 366–382). New York: Guilford Press.

Kerns, K. A., Klepac, L., & Cole, A. K. (1996). Peer relationships and preadolescents' perceptions of security in the child–mother relationship. *Developmental Psychology, 32*(3), 457–466. doi: 10.1037//0012-1649.32.3.457

Kerns, K. A., & Richardson, R. A. (Eds.). (2005). *Attachment in middle childhood.* New York: Guilford Press.

Kerr, M., & Stattin, H. (2000). What parents know, how they know it, and several forms of adolescent adjustment: Further support for a reinterpretation of monitoring. *Developmental Psychology, 36*(3), 366–380. doi: 10.1037/0012-1649.36.3.366

Kestenbaum, R., Farber, E., & Sroufe, L. A. (1989). Individual differences in empathy among preschoolers' concurrent and predictive validity. In N. Eisenberg, (Ed.), *New Directions for Child Development Series: No. 44. Empathy and related emotional responses* (pp. 51–56). San Francisco: Jossey-Bass.

Khaleque, A., & Rohner, R. P. (2002). Perceived parental acceptance–rejection and psychological adjustment: A meta-analysis of cross-cultural and intracultural studies. *Journal of Marriage and the Family, 64*, 54–64. doi: 10.1111/j.1741-3737.2002.00054.x

Kiang, L., Moreno, A. J., & Robinson, J. L., (2004). Maternal preconceptions about parenting predict child temperament, maternal sensitivity, and children's empathy. *Developmental Psychology, 40*, 1081–1092.

Kohlberg, L., Ricks, D., & Snarey, J. (1984). Childhood development as a predictor of adaptation in adulthood. *Genetic Psychology Monographs, 110*, 94–162.

Kopp, C. B. (1989). Regulation of distress and negative emotions: A developmental view. *Developmental Psychology, 25*, 343–354. doi: 10.1037//0012-1649.25.3.343

Kuczynski, L., Harach, L., & Bernardini, S. C. (1999). Psychology's child meets sociology's child: Agency, power and influence in parent–child relations. In C. Shehan (Ed.), *Through the eyes of the child: Revisioning children as active agents of family life* (pp. 21–52). Stamford, CT: JAI Press.

Ladd, G. W., Kochenderfer, B. J., & Coleman, C. C. (1996). Friendship quality as a predictor of young children's early school adjustment. *Child Development, 67*, 1103–1118. doi: 10.1111/j.1467-8624.1996.tb01785.x

Ladd, G. W., & Proffitt, S. M. (1996). The Child Behavior Scale: A teacher-report measure of young children's aggressive, withdrawn, and prosocial behaviors. *Developmental Psychology, 32*, 1008–1024. doi: 10.1037//0012-1649.32.6.1008

Landau, S., Milich, R., & Whitten, P. (1994). A comparison of teacher and peer assessment of social status. *Journal of Clinical Child Psychology, 13*, 44–49.

Landreth, G. L., & Lobaugh, A. F. (1998). Filial therapy with incarcerated fathers: Effects on parental acceptance of child, parental stress, and child adjustment. *Journal of Counseling & Development, 76*, 157–165.

Lipsey, M. W., & Derzon, J. H. (1998). Predictors of violent or serious delinquency in adolescence and early adulthood: A synthesis of longitudinal research. In R. Loeber & D. P. Farrington (Eds.), *Serious & violent juvenile offenders: Risk factors and successful interventions* (pp. 86–105). Thousand Oaks, CA: SAGE.

Loeber, R., Stouthamer-Loeber, M., & Green, S. M. (1991). Age of onset of problem behavior in boys, and later disruptive and delinquent behavior. *Criminal Behavior and Mental Health, 1*, 229–246.

Loper, A. B., Carlson, L. W., Levitt, L., & Scheffel, K. (2009). Parenting stress, alliance, child contact, and adjustment of imprisoned mothers and fathers. *Journal of Offender Rehabilitation*, **48**, 483–503. doi: 10.1080/10509670903081300

Loper, A. B., & Levitt, L. (2010). Mental health needs of female offenders. In T. J. Fagan & R. K. Ax (Eds.), *Correctional mental health: From theory to best practice* (pp. 213–234). New York: SAGE.

Loper, A. B., & Novero, C. M. (2010). Parenting programs for prisoners: Current research and new directions. In J. M. Eddy & J. Poehlmann (Eds.), *Children of incarcerated parents: A handbook for researchers and practitioners* (pp. 189–215). Washington, DC: Urban Institute Press.

Lopez, C., & Bhat, C. S. (2007). Supporting students with incarcerated parents in schools: A group intervention. *Journal for Specialists in Group Work*, **32**, 139–153. doi: 10.1080/01933920701227125

Lotze, G. M., Ravindran, N., & Myers, B. J. (2010). Moral emotions, emotion self-regulation callous-unemotional traits and problem behavior in children of incarcerated mothers. *Journal of Child and Family Studies*, **19**, 702–713. doi: 10.1007/s10826-010-9358-7

Luthar, S. S., Cicchetti, D., & Becker, B. (2000). The construct of resilience: A critical evaluation and guidelines for future work. *Child Development*, **71**, 543–562. doi: 10.1111/1467-8624.00164

Maccoby, E. E., & Martin, J. (1983). *Socialization in the context of the family: Parent–child interaction* (4th ed., Vol. 4). New York: John Wiley & Sons.

Mackintosh, V. H., Myers, B. J., & Kennon, S. S. (2006). Children of incarcerated mothers and their caregivers: Factors affecting the quality of their relationship. *Journal of Child and Family Studies*, **15**(5), 581–596. doi: 10.1007/s10826-006-9030-4

Magnusson, D., & Torestad, B. (1993). A holistic view of personality: A model revisited. *Annual Review of Psychology*, **44**, 427–452. doi: 10.1146/annurev.psych.44.1.427

Main, M., & Goldwyn, R. (1998). *Adult attachment classification system.* Unpublished manuscript, University of California, Berkeley, CA.

Main, M., Kaplan, N., & Cassidy, J. (1985). Security in infancy, childhood and adulthood: A move to the level of representation. In I. Bretherton & E. Waters (Eds.), Growing points in attachment theory and research [Monograph]. *Monographs of the Society for Research in Child Development* (Vol. 50, 1–2, Serial No. 209; 66–104).

Makariev, D., & Shaver, P. R. (2010). Attachment, parental incarceration and possibilities for intervention: An overview. *Attachment and Human Development*, **12**, 311–331. doi: 10.1080/14751790903416939

Maruschak, L. M., Glaze, L. E., & Mumola, C. J. (2010). Incarcerated parents and their children: Findings from the Bureau of Justice Statistics. In J. M. Eddy & J. Poehlmann (Eds.), *Children of incarcerated parents: A handbook for researchers and practitioners* (pp. 33–54). Washington, DC: Urban Institute Press.

Masten, A. S. (2001). Ordinary magic: Resilience processes in development. *American Psychologist*, **56**, 227–238. doi: 10.1037//0003-066X.56.3.227

Masten, A. S., & Obradovic, J. (2006). Competence and resilience in development. *Annals of New York Academy of Sciences*, **1094**, 13–27. doi: 10.1196/annals.1376.003

Maughan, A., & Cicchetti, D. (2002). The impact of child maltreatment and interadult violence on children's emotion regulation abilities. *Child Development*, **73**, 1525–1542. doi: 10.1111/1467-8624.00488

McConnell, M. C., & Kerig, P. K. (2002). Assessing coparenting in families of school-age children: Validation of the coparenting and family rating system. *Canadian Journal of Behavioural Science*, **34**, 44–58. doi: 10.1037/h0087154

McCord, J. (1991). Questioning the value of punishment. *Social Problems*, **38**(2), 167–179. doi: 10.1525/sp.1991.38.2.03a00040

McHale, J. (1995). Coparenting and triadic interactions during infancy: The roles of marital distress and child gender. *Developmental Psychology*, **31**, 985–996. doi: 10.1037/0012-1649.31.6.985

McHale, J. P. (2007). When infants grow up in multiperson relationship systems. *Infant Mental Health Journal*, **28**, 370–392. doi: 10.1002/imhj.20142

McHale, J., & Fivaz-Depeursinge, E. (1999). Understanding triadic and family group process during infancy and early childhood. *Clinical Child and Family Psychology Review*, **2**, 107–127. doi: 10.1023/A:1021847714749

McHale, J., Khazan, I., Erera, P., Rotman, T., DeCourcey, W., & McConnell, M. (2002). Coparenting in diverse family systems. In M. Bornstein (Ed.), *Handbook of parenting: Vol. 3: Being and becoming a parent* (pp. 75–107). Mahwah, NJ: Erlbaum.

McHale, J., Kuersten-Hogan, R., & Lauretti, A. (2000). Evaluating coparenting and family-level dynamics during infancy and early childhood: The Coparenting and Family Rating System. In P. Kerig & K. Lindahl (Eds.), *Family observational coding systems: Resources for systemic research* (pp. 151–170). NJ: Erlbaum.

McHale, J., & Lindahl, K. (2011). *Coparenting: A clinical and conceptual look at family systems*. Washington, DC: American Psychological Association Press.

Measelle, J., Ablow, J., Cowan, P., & Cowan, C. (1998). Assessing young children's views of their academic, social, and emotional lives: An evaluation of self-perception scales of the Berkeley Puppet Interview. *Child Development*, **69**, 1556–1576. doi: 10.1111/j.1467-8624.1998.tb06177.x

Mikulincer, M., & Florian, V. (1997). Are emotional and instrumental supportive interactions beneficial in times of stress? The impact of attachment style. *Anxiety, Stress, and Coping*, **10**, 109–127. doi: 10.1080/10615809708249297

Miller, K. M. (2006). The impact of parental incarceration on children: An emerging need for effective interventions. *Child and Adolescent Social Work Journal*, **23**, 472–486. doi: 10.1007/s10560-006-0065-6

Mills, C. B., & Carwile, A. M. (2009). The good, the bad, and the borderline: Separating teasing from bullying. *Communication Education*, **58**, 276–301.

Minuchin, S. (1974). *Families and family therapy*. Cambridge, MA: Harvard Press.

Minuchin, P., Colapinto, J., Minuchin, S., & Munichin, S. (2007). *Working with families of the poor*. New York: Guilford Press.

Moffitt, T. E. (1993). Adolescence-limited and life-course-persistent antisocial behavior: A developmental taxonomy. *Psychological Review*, **100**, 674–701. doi: 10.1037//0033-295X.100.4.674

Morris, A. S., Silk, J. S., Steinberg, L., Myers, S. S., & Robinson, L. R. (2007). Role of the family context in the development of emotion regulation. *Social Development*, **16**, 361–388. doi: 10.1111/j.1467-9507.2007.00389.x

Mumola, C. J. (2000). *Incarcerated parents and their children*. Washington, DC: U.S. Department of Justice. Retrieved from http://www.ojp.usdoj.gov/bjs/pub/pdf/iptc.pdf

Murray, J. (2010). Longitudinal research on the effects of parental incarceration on children. In J. M. Eddy & J. Poehlmann (Eds.), *Children of incarcerated parents: A handbook for researchers and practitioners* (pp. 55–74). Washington, DC: Urban Institute Press.

Murray, J., & Farrington, D. P. (2005). Parental imprisonment: Effects on boys' antisocial behaviour and delinquency through the life course. *Journal of Child Psychology and Psychiatry*, **46**, 1269–1278. doi: 10.1111/j.1469-7610.2005.01433.x

Murray, J., Farrington, D. P., Sekol, I., & Olsen, R. F. (2009). Effects of parental imprisonment on child antisocial behaviour and mental health: A systematic review. *Campbell Systematic Reviews*, **4**, 1–105. Oslo, Norway: Campbell Collaboration. http://www.ncjrs.gov/pdffiles1/nij/grants/229378.pdf

Murray, J., & Farrington, D. P. (2008). The effects of parental imprisonment on children. In M. Tony (Ed.), *Crime and justice: A review of research* (Vol. 37, pp. 133–206). Chicago: University of Chicago Press.

Murray, J., & Murray, L. (2010). Parental incarceration, attachment, and child psychopathology. *Attachment and Human Development*, **12**, 289–309. doi: 10.1080/14751790903416889

Myers, B. J., Smarsh, T., Amlund-Hagen, K., & Kennon, S. (1999). Children of incarcerated mothers. *Journal of Child and Family Studies*, **8**, 11–25. doi: 10.1023/A:1022990410036

National Institute of Child Health and Human Development. (2001). *Bullying widespread in U.S. schools, survey finds*. Washington, DC: National Institutes of Health.

Nesmith, A., & Ruhland, E. (2008). Children of incarcerated parents: Challenges and resiliency, in their own words. *Children and Youth Services Review*, **30**, 1119–1130. doi: 10.1016/j.childyouth.2008.02.006

Olson, D., Portner, J., & Lavee, Y. (1985). *Family adaptability and cohesion evaluation scales III*. St. Paul: University of Minnesota.

Olweus, D. (1979). Stability of aggressive reaction patterns in males: A review. *Psychological Bulletin*, **86**, 852–875. doi: 10.1037/0033-2909.86.4.852

Olweus, D. (1993). *Bullying at school: What we know and what we can do*. Cambridge, MA: Blackwell.

Olweus, D. (2006). Bullying at school: Knowledge base and an effective intervention program. *Annals of the New York Academy of Sciences*, **795**, 265–276.

Owen, M. T., & Cox, M. J. (1997). Marital conflict and the development of infant–parent attachment relationships. *Journal of Family Psychology*, **11**, 152–164. doi: 10.1037/0893-3200.11.2.152

Parke, R. D., & Clarke-Stewart, K. A. (2001). *Effects of parental incarceration on young children*. Paper presented at the National Policy Conference, From Prison to Home: The Effect of Incarceration and Reentry on Children, Families and Communities. National Institutes of Health, Bethesda, MD.

Parmar, P., & Rohner, R. P. (2005). Relations among perceived intimate partner acceptance, remembered parental acceptance–rejection, and psychological adjustment among young adults in India. *Ethos*, **33**, 402–413. doi: 10.1525/eth.2005.33.3.402

Patterson, G. R. (1982). Observations of family process. In G. R. Patterson (Ed.), *Coercive family process: A social learning approach* (Vol. 3, pp. 41–65). Eugene, OR: Castalia.

Patterson, G. R., Capaldi, D. C., & Bank, L. (1991). An early starter model for predicting delinquency. In D. J. Pepler & K. H. Rubin (Eds.), *The development and treatment of childhood aggression*. Hillsdale, NJ: Erlbaum.

Patterson, G. R., Reid, J. B., & Dishion, T. J. (1992). *A social learning approach: Antisocial boys* (Vol. IV). Eugene, OR: Castalia.

Pellegrini, A. D., & Bartini, M. (2000). A longitudinal study of bullying, victimization, and peer affiliation during the transition from primary school to middle school. *American Educational Research Journal*, **37**, 699–725.

Pew Charitable Trusts. (2008). *1 in 100: Behind bars in America 2008*. Philadelphia: Author.

Phillips, S. D., Burns, B. J., Wagner, R. H., & Barth, R. P. (2004). Parental arrest and children involved with child welfare services agencies. *American Journal of Orthopsychiatry*, **74**(2), 174–186. doi: 10.1037/.74.2.174

Phillips, S. D., & Erkanli, A. (2008). Differences in patterns of maternal arrest and the parent, family, and child problems encountered in working with families. *Children and Youth Services Review*, **30**(2), 157–172. doi: 10.1016/j.childyouth.2007.09.003

Phillips, S. D., Erkanli, A., Costello, E. J., & Angold, A. (2006). Differences among children whose mothers have been in contact with the criminal justice system. *Women and Criminal Justice*, **17**, 43–61. doi: 10.1300/J012v17n02_04

Phillips, S. D., Erkanli, A., Keeler, G., Costello, E. J., & Angold, A. (2006). Disentangling the risks: Parent criminal justice involvement and children's exposure to family risks. *Criminology and Public Policy*, **5**, 677–702.

Poehlmann, J. (2003). An attachment perspective on grandparents raising their very young grandchildren: Implications for intervention and research. *Infant Mental Health Journal*, **24**, 149–173. doi: 10.1002/imhj.10047

Poehlmann, J. (2005a). Representations of attachment relationships in children of incarcerated mothers. *Child Development*, **76**, 679–696. doi: 10.1111/j.1467-8624.2005.00871.x

Poehlmann, J. (2005b). Incarcerated mothers' contact with children, perceived family relationships, and depressive symptoms. *Journal of Family Psychology*, **19**, 350–357. doi: 10.1037/0893-3200.19.3.350

Poehlmann, J. (2010). Attachment in infants and children of incarcerated parents. In J. M. Eddy & J. Poehlmann (Eds.), *Children of incarcerated parents: A handbook for researchers and practitioners* (pp. 75–100). Washington DC: Urban Institute Press.

Poehlmann, J., Dallaire, D., Loper, A. B., & Shear, L. D. (2010). Children's contact with their incarcerated parents: Research findings and recommendations. *American Psychologist*, **65**, 575–598. doi: 10.1037/a0020279

Poehlmann, J., & Eddy, J. M. (2010). A research and intervention agenda. In J. M. Eddy & J. Poehlmann (Eds.), *Children of incarcerated parents: A handbook for researchers and practitioners* (pp. 319–342). Washington DC: Urban Institute Press.

Poehlmann, J., Park, J., Bouffiou, L., Abrahams, J., Shlafer, R., & Hahn, E. (2008). Attachment representations in children raised by their grandparents. *Attachment and Human Development*, **10**, 165–188. doi: 10.1080/14616730802113695

Poehlmann, J., Shlafer, R. J., Maes, E., & Hanneman, A. (2008). Factors associated with young children's opportunities for maintaining family relationships during maternal incarceration. *Family Relations*, **57**, 267–280. doi: 10.1111/j.1741-3729.2008.00499.x

Rabe-Hesketh, S., & Skrondal, A. (2008). *Multilevel and longitudinal modeling using stata* (2nd ed.). College Station, TX: Stata Press.

Radloff, L. S. (1977). The CES-D scale: A self-report depression scale for research in the general population. *Applied Psychological Measurement*, **1**, 385–401. doi: 10.1177/014662167700100306

Reid, J. B., & Eddy, J. M. (1997). The prevention of antisocial behavior: Some considerations in the search for effective interventions. In D. M. Stoff, J. Breiling, & J. D. Maser (Eds.), *Handbook of antisocial behavior* (pp. 343–356). New York: John Wiley & Sons.

Reid, J. B., Patterson, G. R., & Snyder, J. (Eds.). (2002). *Antisocial behavior in children and adolescents: A developmental analysis and model for intervention.* Washington, DC: American Psychological Association.

Robins, L. N. (1966). *Deviant children grown up: A sociological and psychiatric study of sociopathic personality.* Baltimore, MD: Williams & Wilkins.

Robins, L. N. (1978). Sturdy childhood predictors of adult antisocial behavior: Replications from longitudinal studies. *Psychological Medicine, 8,* 611–622.

Robinson, J., & Little, C. (1994) Emotional availability in mother-twin dyads: Effects on the organization of relationships. *Psychiatry: Interpersonal and Biological Processes, 57,* 222–231.

Rohner, R. P. (2005). Parental acceptance–rejection questionnaire (PARQ): Test manual. In R. P. Rohner & A. Khaleque (Eds.), *Handbook for the study of parental acceptance and rejection* (4th ed., pp. 43–106). Storrs, CT: Rohner Research Publications.

Rohner, R. P., Khaleque, A., & Cournoyer, D. E. (2005). Parental acceptance–rejection theory, methods, evidence, and implications. In R. P. Rohner & A. Khaleque (Eds.), *Handbook for the study of parental acceptance and rejection* (4th ed., pp. 1–36). Storrs, CT: Rohner Research Publications.

Roisman, G. I., Holland, A., Fortuna, K., Fraley, R. C., Clausell, E., & Clarke, A. (2007). The adult attachment interview and self-reports of attachment style: An empirical rapprochement. *Journal of Personality and Social Psychology, 92,* 678–697. doi: 10.1037/0022-3514.92.4.678

Rose-Krasnor, L. (1997). The nature of social competence: A theoretical review. *Social development, 6,* 111–135.

Rubin, K. H., Bukowski, W., & Parker, J. G. (1998). Peer interactions, relationships and groups. In W. Damon & N. Eisenberg (Eds.), *Handbook of child psychology* (Vol. 3, 5th ed., pp. 619–700). Hoboken, NJ: John Wiley & Sons.

Rutter, M. (1989). Pathways from childhood to adult life. *Journal of Child Psychology and Psychiatry, 30,* 23–51. doi: 10.1111/j.1469-7610.1989.tb00768.x

Rutter, M. (2006). Implications of resilience concepts for scientific understanding. *Annals of the New York Academy of Sciences, 1094,* 1–12. doi: 10.1196/annals.1376.002

Saarni, C. (1999). *The development of emotional competence.* New York: Guilford Press.

Saarni, C., Mumme, D. L., & Campos, J. J. (1998). Emotional development: Action, communication, and understanding. In W. Damon & N. Eisenberg (Eds.), *The handbook of child psychology* (Vol. 3, 5th ed., pp. 237–309). New York: John Wiley & Sons.

Sameroff, A. J. (2000). Dialectical processes in developmental psychopathology. In A. Sameroff, M. Lewis & S. Miller (Eds.), *Handbook of developmental psychopathology* (2nd ed., pp. 23–40). New York: Kluwer Academic/Plenum.

Scambler, D. J., Harris, M. J., & Milich, R. (1998). Sticks and stones: Evaluations of responses to childhood teasing. *Social Development, 7,* 234–249. doi: 10.1111/1467-9507.00064

Schaefer, E. S. (1965). Children's reports of parental behavior: An inventory. *Child Development, 36,* 413–424. doi: 10.2307/1126465

Schiffmann, T., Eddy, J. M., Martinez, C. R., Leve, L., & Newton, R. (2008). *Parenting inside out: Parent management training for incarcerated parents in prison.* Portland, OR: Oregon Social Learning Center and Children's Justice Alliance.

Schneider, B. H., Atkinson, L., & Tardif, C. (2001). Child–parent attachment and children's peer relations: A quantitative review. *Developmental Psychology*, **37**(1), 86–100. doi: http://dx.doi.org/10.1037/0012-1649.37.1.86

Schonert-Reichl, K. A., & Scott, F. (2009). Effectiveness of "The Roots of Empathy" program in promoting children's emotional and social competence: A summary of research findings. In M. Gordon (Ed.), *The roots of empathy: Changing the world child by child* (pp. 239–252). Toronto, Ontario: Thomas Allen.

Shapiro, J. P., Baumeister, R. F., & Kessler, J. W. (1991). A three-component model of children's teasing: Aggression, humor, and ambiguity. *Journal of Social and Clinical Psychology*, **10**, 459–471. doi: 10.1521/jscp.1991.10.4.459

Sheras, P. L., Abindin, R. R., & Konold, T. R. (1998). *Stress index for parents of adolescents professional manual.* Odessa, FL: Psychological Assessment Resources.

Shields, A., & Cicchetti, D. (1997). Emotion regulation among school-age children: The development and validation of a new criterion Q-sort scale. *Developmental Psychology*, **33**, 906–916. doi: 10.1037//0012-1649.33.6.906

Shields, A., & Cicchetti, D. (2001). Parental maltreatment and emotion dysregulation as risk factors for bullying and victimization in middle childhood. *Journal of Clinical Child Psychology*, **30**, 349–363. doi: 10.1207/S15374424JCCP3003_7

Shields, A., Ryan, R. M., & Cicchetti, D. (2001). Narrative representations of caregivers and emotional dysregulation as predictors of maltreated children's rejection by peers. *Developmental Psychology*, **37**, 321–337. doi: 10.1037/0012-1649.37.3.321

Shlafer, R. J., & Poehlmann, J. (2010). Attachment and caregiving relationships in families affected by parental incarceration. *Attachment and Human Development*, **12**, 395–415. doi: 10.1080/14616730903417052

Shlafer, R. J., Poehlmann, J., & Donelan-McCall, N. (2011). Maternal jail time, conviction, and arrest as predictors of children's 15 year antisocial outcomes in the context of a nurse home visiting program. *Journal of Clinical Child and Adolescent Psychology*, **41**, 38–52. doi: 10.1080/15374416.2012.632345

Siegelman, M. (1965). Evaluation of Bronfenbrenner's questionnaire for children concerning parental behavior. *Child Development*, **36**, 163–174. doi: 10.1111/j.1467-8624.1965.tb05290.x

Simpson, J. A., Winterheld, H. A., Rholes, W. S., & Orina, M. M. (2007). Working models of attachment and reactions to different forms of caregiving from romantic partners. *Journal of Personality and Social Psychology*, **93**, 466–477. doi: 10.1037/0022-3514.93.3.466

Smith, A., Krisman, K., Strozier, A. L., & Marley, M. A. (2004). Breaking through the bars: Exploring the experiences of addicted incarcerated parents whose children are cared for by relatives. *Families in Society*, **85**, 187–200. Retrieved from http://flkin.org/images/breaking_thru_bars.pdf

Solomon, D., Battistich, V., Watson, M., & Schaps, E. (2000). A six-district study of educational change: Direct and mediated effects of the Child Development Project. *Social Psychology of Education*, **4**, 3–51. doi: 10.1023/A:1009609606692

Spanier, G. B. (1976). Measuring dyadic adjustment: New scales for assessing the quality of marriage and similar dyads. *Journal of Marriage and the Family*, **38**, 15–28. doi: 10.2307/350547

Speltz, M. L., DeKlyen, M., & Greenberg, M. T. (1999). Attachment in boys with early onset conduct problems. *Development and Psychopathology*, **11**(2), 269–285. doi: 10.1017/S0954579499002059

Sroufe, L. A. (1989). Relationships, self and indivdual adaptation. In A. J. Sameroff & R. N. Emde (Eds.), *Relationship Disturbances in Early Childhood.* New York: Basic Books.

StataCorp. (2009). *Stata: Release 11.* Statistical Software. College Station, TX: StataCorp.

Strozier, A., Armstrong, M., Skuza, S., Cecil, D., & McHale, J. (2011). Coparenting in kinship families with an incarcerated mother: A qualitative study. *Families in Society,* **92,** 55–61.

Tabachnik, B. G., & Fidell, L. S. (2001). *Using multivariate statistics.* (4th ed.). Boston: Allyn and Bacon.

Talbot, J. A., Baker, J. K., & McHale, J. P. (2009). Sharing the love: Prebirth adult attachment status and coparenting adjustment during early infancy. *Parenting: Science and Practice,* **9,** 56–77. doi: 10.1080/15295190802656760

Terry, R., & Cole, J. D. (1991). A comparison of methods for defining sociometric status. *Developmental Psychology,* **27,** 867–880. doi: 10.1037//0012-1649.27.5.867

The Sentencing Project. (2009). The sentencing project: Drug policy. Retrieved November 30, 2009, from http://www.sentencingproject.org/template/page.cfm?id=128

Thompson, R. A. (2008). Attachment-related mental representations: Introduction to the special issue. *Attachment and Human Development,* **10,** 347–358. doi: 10.1080/14616730802461334

Thompson, R. A., & Meyer, S. (2007). Socialization of emotion regulation in the family. In J. J. Gross (Ed.), *Handbook of Emotion Regulation* (pp. 249–268). New York: The Guilford Press.

Travis, J., & Waul, M. (2003). *Prisoners once removed: The impact of incarceration and reentry on children, families, and communities.* Washington, DC: Urban Institute Press.

Trice, A. D., & Brewster, J. (2004). The effects of maternal incarceration on adolescent children. *Journal of Police and Criminal Psychology,* **19,** 27–35. doi: 10.1007/BF02802572

Tuerk, E. H., & Loper, A. B. (2006). Contact between incarcerated mothers and their children: Assessing parenting stress. *Journal of Offender Rehabilitation,* **43,** 23–43. doi: 10.1300/J076v43n01_02

U.S. Bureau of Justice Statistics. (2007). *Probation and parole in the United States, 2006.* Retrieved from November 28, 2008, http://www.ojp.usdoj.gov/bjs/pandp.htm

Veneziano, R. A., & Rohner, R. P. (1998). Perceived paternal acceptance, paternal involvement, and youths' psychological adjustment in a rural, biracial southern community. *Journal of Marriage and the Family,* **60,** 335–343. doi: 10.2307/353852

Vinik, J., Almas, A., & Grusec, J. (2011). Mothers' knowledge of what distresses and what comforts their children predicts children's coping, empathy, and prosocial behavior. *Parenting: Science and Practice,* **11,** 56–71. doi: 10.1080/15295192.2011.539508

Voss, L. S. (1997). Teasing, disputing, and playing: Cross-gender interactions and space utilization among first and third graders. *Gender and Society,* **11,** 238–256.

Walker, H. M., Shinn, M. R., O'Neill, R. E., & Ramsey, E. (1987). A longitudinal assessment of the development of antisocial behavior in boys: Rationale, methodology, and first-year results. *Remedial and Special Education,* **8,** 7–16. doi: 10.1177/074193258700800403

Warden, D., & Mackinnon, S. (2003). Prosocial children, bullies and victims: An investigation of their sociometric status, empathy and social problem-solving strategies. *British Journal of Developmental Psychology,* **21,** 367–385. doi: 10.1348/026151003322277757

Warm, T. R. (1997). The role of teasing in development and vice versa. *Developmental and Behavioral Pediatrics,* **18,** 97–101. doi: 10.1097/00004703-199704000-00004

Werner, E. E. (1993). Risk, resilience, and recover: Perspective from the Kauai Longitudinal Study. *Development and Psychopathology,* **5,** 503–515.

West, H. C., & Sabol, W. J. (2008). *Prisoners in 2007.* NCJ 224280. Washington, DC: U.S. Department of Justice, Bureau of Justice Statistics.

Western, B., & Wildeman, C. (2009). The Black family and mass incarceration. *The ANNALS of the American Academy of Political and Social Science,* **621**, 221–242. doi: 10.1177/0002716208324850

Wilbur, M. B., Marani, J. E., Appugliese, D., Woods, R., Siegal, J. A., Cabral, H. J., et al. (2007). Socioemotional effects of fathers' incarceration on low-income, urban, school-aged children. *Pediatrics,* **120**, 678–685. doi: 10.1542/peds.2006-2166

Wilczak, G. L., & Markstrom, C. A. (1999). The effects of parent education on parental locus of control and satisfaction of incarcerated fathers. *International Journal of Offender Therapy and Comparative Criminology,* **43**, 90–102. doi: 10.1177/0306624X99431009

Wildeman, C. (2009). Parental imprisonment, the prison boom, and the concentration of childhood disadvantage. *Demography,* **46**, 265–280.

Windle, M. (1992). A longitudinal study of stress buffering for adolescent problem behaviors. *Developmental Psychology,* **28**, 522–530. doi: 10.1037/0012-1649.28.3.522

Young, D. S., & Smith, C. J. (2000). When moms are incarcerated: The needs of children, mothers, and caregivers. *Families in Society: The Journal of Contemporary Human Services,* **81** (2), 130–141.

Zahn-Waxler, C., Robinson, J. L., & Emde, R. N. (1992). The development of empathy in twins. *Developmental Psychology,* **28**, 1038–1047. doi: 10.1037//0012-1649.28.6.1038

Zoccolillo, M., Pickles, A., Quinton, D., & Rutter, M. (1992). The outcome of childhood conduct disorder: Implications for defining antisocial personality disorder and conduct disorder. *Psychological Medicine,* **22**, 971–986. doi: 10.1017/S003329170003854X

ACKNOWLEDGMENTS

Correspondence about this monograph should be directed to Julie Poehlmann, Ph.D., Professor and Chair, Human Development and Family Studies, Waisman Center, University of Wisconsin, 1500 Highland Avenue, Madison, WI 53705; 608-263-4839; E-mail: poehlmann@waisman.wisc.edu. Special thanks to the many incarcerated parents, their children, and the caregivers of their children from around the U.S. who participated in the various studies assembled here. We are appreciative of the diverse disciplines, research methods, and scientific teams represented in this monograph, and of the different perspectives each brings to understanding the children of incarcerated parents and their families. We are thankful to have the opportunity to work on this project together, and for the support and patience of our families as we endeavored to complete this volume. Funding from a variety of sources supported the studies in this monograph. The work of James McHale and colleagues was supported by Grant No. HD050730 from the NICHD, U.S. PHS. The work of J. Mark Eddy and colleagues was supported by Grant No. MH46690 from the Division of Epidemiology and Services Research, NIMH & ORMH, U.S. PHS; Grant No. MH65553 from the Division of Epidemiology and Services Research, NIMH, NIH, U.S. PHS; a grant from the Edna McConnell Clark Foundation; and funding from the State of Oregon.

CONTRIBUTORS

Al M. Best, Ph.D., is an Associate Professor in the School of Dentistry at Virginia Commonwealth University. His research interests include the design and analysis of multivariate experiments as well as data management and graphical methods.

Bert Burraston, Ph.D., is an Assistant Professor in the Department of Criminology and Criminal Justice at the University of Memphis. He is a quantitative methodologist and sociologist and has extensive experience working with longitudinal data sets. His research focuses on the development of antisocial behavior and child neglect and abuse. He has conducted a variety of studies using new technologies to improve services within the juvenile justice system.

Dawn K. Cecil, Ph.D., is an Associate Professor of Criminology at the University of South Florida St. Petersburg. Her research focuses on issues related to incarceration in the United States, including incarcerated mothers, as well as images of incarceration and its effect on people's perceptions.

Danielle H. Dallaire, Ph.D., is an Associate Professor of Psychology at The College of William and Mary. She received her Ph.D. from Temple University in 2003. Her research interests include children's social and emotional development and promoting resilience in children and families in high-risk environments, particularly those dealing with parental incarceration.

J. Mark Eddy, Ph.D., is the Director of Research at Partners for Our Children in the School of Social Work at the University of Washington, and a licensed psychologist. His work focuses on the development and testing of research-based interventions designed to prevent child abuse and neglect and childhood antisocial behavior and related problem behaviors. He has served as principal investigator on several longitudinal randomized controlled trials of interventions within various systems of care, including adult corrections, juvenile justice, child welfare, and primary school.

Maria I. Kuznetsova, Ph.D., is an Assistant Professor of Psychology at the University of Wyoming. Her research focuses on adoptions, including the longer term adjustment of children and adolescents from eastern European countries who have been adopted into U.S. families.

Geri M. Lotze, Ph.D., is an Assistant Professor of Psychology at Virginia Commonwealth University. In addition to her interest in children impacted by maternal incarceration, her scholarship focuses on the impact of disabilities throughout the lifespan and related issues, including healthcare service provision for children, violence prevention in adolescence, and stress and coping during emerging adulthood.

Ann Booker Loper, Ph. D., is a clinical psychologist and Professor at the University of Virginia's Curry School of Education. Her research focuses on mental health and adjustment of prisoners, with a particular interest in understanding the experiences of incarcerated parents and their families. Dr. Loper has collaborated with prison, jail, and community partners in the development of a parenting program for incarcerated mothers, and is currently undertaking an evaluation of jail transitional programming. She has also conducted research concerning the needs and characteristics of female juvenile offenders.

Virginia H. Mackintosh, Ph.D., is an Assistant Professor of Psychology at the University of Mary Washington. Her research interests carry the common thread of families trying to function in the face of difficult challenges. She has worked with children of incarcerated mothers, giving special attention to the grandparent caregivers, and has taught parenting classes within prisons.

Charles R. Martinez Jr., Ph.D., is the Director of the Center for Equity Promotion and an Associate Professor in the College of Education at the University of Oregon. His work centers on identifying factors that promote healthy adjustment for children and parents following stressful life events, taking into consideration the cultural context. He has led numerous NIH-funded research projects designed to examine risk and protective factors involved in linking acculturation to behavioral health outcomes for Latino families and to develop and test culturally specific interventions for Latino families at risk of behavioral health problems. He is a licensed psychologist.

James P. McHale, Ph.D., is Professor and Chair of the Department of Psychology and Director of the Family Study Center at University of South Florida St. Petersburg, and former Director of Clinical Training at Clark University in Worcester, MA. His studies of early infant, child, and family adjustment have been grant-supported by the National Institutes of Health since 1996, and his 2007 work *Charting the Bumpy Road of Coparenthood* received the Irving B. Harris National Book Award from the Zero to Three Press.

Barbara J. Myers, Ph.D., is an Associate Professor and Director of the doctoral program in Developmental Psychology at Virginia Commonwealth University. Her research focuses on two groups of high-risk children and families: children with autism and children affected by parental incarceration. She serves as the chair of the Board of Juvenile Justice for the Commonwealth of Virginia.

Caitlin Novero Clarke, M.Ed., is a doctoral student in the Clinical and School Psychology Program at the Curry School of Education, University of Virginia. She has worked with forensic populations in prison rehabilitation programs in Boston, MA, and Central Virginia.

Julie Poehlmann, Ph.D., is Professor and Chair of the Human Development and Family Studies department at the University of Wisconsin-Madison; an investigator at the Waisman Center, an affiliate of the Institute for Research on Poverty; and a licensed psychologist. She is also the Director of the Center for Child and Family Well-Being at the University of Wisconsin. Through numerous publications and outreach efforts, she has brought the attention of the child development and family studies communities to the issue of parental incarceration. Her research with children of incarcerated parents has been funded by the National Institutes of Health and the Department of Health and Human Services. She also serves as an advisor to Sesame Street as part of their resilience initiative.

Neeraja Ravindran, Ph.D., is a postdoctoral fellow at the Carolina Institute for Developmental Disabilities, University of North Carolina School of Medicine, where she provides clinical diagnostic services to children with autism and other developmental disabilities. Her research examines cultural perspectives on health, health problems, and disabilities. In particular, she is interested in parent and professional beliefs about and treatments for autism spectrum disorders in southern India.

Selin Salman, M.S., is a doctoral candidate in Social Psychology at Middle East Technical University (METU), Turkey. Her scholarly work bridges interests in attachment, maternal sensitivity, parenting, child adjustment, family assessment, and family issues.

Anne Strozier, Ph.D., MSW, is an Associate Professor in the School of Social Work at the University of South Florida and a licensed psychologist. Dr. Strozier founded the Florida Kinship Center located in the School of Social

Work. The Center serves as a statewide resource center, establishes and facilitates support groups, develops curriculum, facilitates trainings, and conducts research.

Janice L. Zeman, Ph.D., is a Professor in the Department of Psychology at the College of William and Mary. She received her Ph.D. in 1991 from Vanderbilt University. Her program of research has broadly examined emotion regulation processes in childhood and adolescence with particular emphases on parental and peer socialization of anger and sadness; the role of emotion regulation in the development, maintenance, and exacerbation of internalizing symptomatology; the assessment of emotion in children; and the moderating role of emotion processes in children of high-risk status.

STATEMENT OF EDITORIAL POLICY

The SRCD *Monographs* series aims to publish major reports of developmental research that generates authoritative new findings and that foster a fresh perspective and/or integration of data/research on conceptually significant issues. Submissions may consist of individually or group-authored reports of findings from some single large-scale investigation or from a series of experiments centering on a particular question. Multiauthored sets of independent studies concerning the same underlying question also may be appropriate. A critical requirement in such instances is that the individual authors address common issues and that the contribution arising from the set as a whole be unique, substantial, and well integrated. Manuscripts reporting interdisciplinary or multidisciplinary research on significant developmental questions and those including evidence from diverse cultural, racial, and ethnic groups are of particular interest. Also of special interest are manuscripts that bridge basic and applied developmental science, and that reflect the international perspective of the Society. Because the aim of the *Monographs* series is to enhance cross-fertilization among disciplines or subfields as well as advance knowledge on specialized topics, the links between the specific issues under study and larger questions relating to developmental processes should emerge clearly and be apparent for both general readers and specialists on the topic. In short, irrespective of how it may be framed, work that contributes significant data and/or extends a developmental perspective will be considered.

Potential authors who may be unsure whether the manuscript they are planning wouldmake an appropriate submission to the SRCD *Monographs* are invited to draft an outline or prospectus of what they propose and send it to the incoming editor for review and comment.

Potential authors are not required to be members of the Society for Research in Child Development nor affiliated with the academic discipline of psychology to submit a manuscript for consideration by the *Monographs*. The significance of the work in extending developmental theory and in contributing new empirical information is the crucial consideration.

Submissions should contain a minimum of 80 manuscript pages (including tables and references). The upper boundary of 150–175 pages is more flexible, but authors should try to keep within this limit. If color artwork is submitted, and the authors believe color art is necessary to the presentation of their work, the submissions letter should indicate that one or more authors or their institutions are prepared to pay the substantial costs associated with color art reproduction. Please submit manuscripts electronically to the SRCD *Monographs* Online Submissions and Review Site (Scholar One) at http://mc.manuscriptcentral. com/mono. Please contact the *Monographs* office with any questions at monographs@srcd.org.

The corresponding author for any manuscript must, in the submission letter, warrant that all coauthors are in agreement with the content of the manuscript. The corresponding author also is responsible for informing all coauthors, in a timely manner, of manuscript submission, editorial decisions, reviews received, and any revisions recommended. Before publication, the corresponding author must warrant in the submissions letter that the study has been conducted according to the ethical guidelines of the Society for Research in Child Development.

A more detailed description of all editorial policies, evaluation processes, and format requirements can be found under the "Submission Guidelines" link at http://srcd.org/publications/monographs.

Monographs Editorial Office
e-mail: monographs@srcd.org

Editor, Patricia J. Bauer
Department of Psychology, Emory University
36 Eagle Row
Atlanta, GA 30322
e-mail: pjbauer@emory.edu

Note to NIH Grantees

Pursuant to NIH mandate, Society through Wiley-Blackwell will post the accepted version of Contributions authored by NIH grantholders to PubMed Central upon acceptance. This accepted version will be made publicly available 12 months after publication. For further information, see http://www.wiley.com/go/nihmandate.

SUBJECT INDEX

Page numbers in *italics* refer to figures and tables.

CURRENT